The Jewish Celebrity Cookbook

Milwaukee Jewish Day School

Foreword by Steven Raichlen
Author of *Healthy Jewish Cooking* and *The Barbecue Bible*

Affiliated Publishers in
Milwaukee • Denver • Vancouver, B.C.

Cover and Text Design by Shelby Keefe

05 04 03 02 01 5 4 3 2 1

ISBN: 0-9706531-0-7
Library of Congress Card Number: 00-192990
First Printing January 2001
Printed in the United States of America

All proceeds from the sale of this book benefit
Milwaukee Jewish Day School, Inc.

6401 N. Santa Monica Blvd.
Milwaukee, WI 53217
www.mjds.org

Published by PB Publishing, a division of Printstar Books, Milwaukee, Wisconsin

5630 N. Lake Drive, Milwaukee, Wisconsin 53217
414-906-0600 • e-mail: pbpub@execpc.com
Affiliated Publishers in
Milwaukee • Denver • Vancouver, B.C.

Introduction

Three years ago a small group of dedicated parents began working on this book. Our goal was to raise funds for Milwaukee Jewish Day School, a community day school whose 350 students represent the spectrum of Jewish observance in our Milwaukee community. When we started this project, little did we know what a gargantuan task we were undertaking. Our enthusiasm and hard work carried us through. With the help of students, teachers, staff, and additional parent volunteers, the book has become a reality. We invite you to read and enjoy this outstanding collection of recipes, accompanied by photos, biographies, and anecdotes. Your enjoyment will be increased by the knowledge that all proceeds from the sale of this book benefit Milwaukee Jewish Day School.

Cookbook Committee

Florence Steinberger, Editor

Toby Colton

Wendy Ellis

Donna Glassman

Lisa Gorelick

Susan Gruenberg

Acknowledgments

This book would not have been possible without the assistance of numerous individuals:

For assuring that each recipe is both user friendly and delicious, thank you to recipe testers Mary Aguilu, Debra Altshul-Stark, Susan Armour Seidman, Natanya Blanck, Diane Cocos, Bev Crawford, Liz Crawford, Fran Dunn, Marge Eiseman, Pam Goldner, Alice Greenfield, Jan Kaufman, Carolyn Kimmel, Debby Lev-er, Susan Richheimer, Pam Frydman-Roza, Marilyn Ruby, Cheryl Siegel-Gajewski, Susan Solvang, Nancy Stillman, Barbara Tick, Amy Waldman, and David Mrotek-Waldman.

For their help with researching and writing biographies, thank you to Joan Braune and Nikki and Jack Levine. For typing the often messy and difficult-to-read manuscript, we thank Dick Alpert, Rebecca Feiring, Aura Mollick Hirschman, Anne Kravit, Terri Minkin, and Nikki Skinner. For her editing skills extraordinaire, thank you to Mary Dykstra. For his help with marketing, thank you to Steve Weinstein, and for his web page design, we thank Noah Dermer. Thank you to Susan Pittelman for being more than a publisher and providing invaluable assistance and advice. For sharing her design talents with us, we thank Shelby Keefe, and for her editorial guidance, thank you to Kim Parsons.

We appreciate the patience of the Ready Reference librarians of the Milwaukee Public Library, who answered innumerable questions. A special thank you to Jane Clare for all of her help. Thank you, also, to the students, parents, teachers, and staff of Milwaukee Jewish Day School for helping to compile lists of celebrities, write letters, contact celebrities, publicize and mail books, and, most of all, for their enthusiasm and moral support.

Finally, we'd like to give special thanks to the eighty-seven contributors to this book (and their publicists and assistants) for their generosity in taking time out of their busy lives to help a small Jewish day school.

Milwaukee Jewish Day School gratefully acknowledges the following contributors for helping to make this book possible:

In memory of Valerie Freidel Prager ("Bobby") and her son, Charles Henry Prager

Dinner at our house meant everything—it was the best of times and the worst of times, and it always began at 6:00 p.m.! Education, world issues, and life experiences were served along with the main dish. Nothing was sacred—discussions were lively and disagreements were common.

Our supper meal consisted of delicious Old World foods: beef goulash, sweet and sour cabbage, and "knuckles" (our family version of dumplings). We have precious memories of the competition between Charlie and Bobby vying for the honor of making the best knuckles.

Though Charlie and Bobby are no longer with us, their recipes are prepared for our traditional family meals, and their legacy continues in our hearts (and in our stomachs) forever!

Harriet Prager; Shari, Mike, Marissa, and Matthew Mullen; Renee and John Popkey; David, Diane, Josh, Zak, and Noah Cocos

In honor of Rosa Wajntraub Schaumberg,
in our opinion, the best cook in the world.
With love,
Fred Schaumberg, Lynne Langlois, Jaron Schaumberg, and Austin Schaumberg

To Shira and Orlee,
All our love, Mom and Dad

To Rebecca and Jacob with love,
Mom and Dad

In loving memory of Suzann M. Colton,
Ervin Colton

Nina and Rich Edelman and Family

Tikkun Olam Foundation

Foreword

Jews love food. And Jews love books. These simple truths explain, perhaps, why there are so many great Jewish cookbooks. It gives me great pleasure to introduce the latest addition to the delectable literature of Jewish cookery: *The Jewish Celebrity Cookbook.*

Like most books, this one began with a dream, the dream of a small group of parents, students, and teachers to raise funds for Milwaukee Jewish Day School. A Jewish celebrity cookbook seemed like the perfect fund-raiser: it would appeal to a broad national audience of Jewish readers, hungry cooks, and people interested in celebrities.

The success of the project surpassed the wildest dreams of its creators. Celebrities from all fields—actors, visual artists, writers, musicians, radio and television personalities, sports figures, even an astronomer—rushed to contribute prized personal recipes to the little school in Milwaukee.

In the following pages, you'll learn how to make Itzhak Perlman's Very Fattening Chopped Chicken Livers, Paul Newman's Dilled Fillets of Scrod with Joanne's Hollandaise Sauce, Beverly Sills' "Dutch Babies" Pancake, Barbara Walters' Mother's Stuffed Cabbage Rolls, and Theodore Bikel's Apple Crisp. Your mouth will water as you read about Billy Joel's Grilled Tuna and Marinated Cucumber Salad, Leon Uris' Osso Buco, and Abigail "Dear Abby" Van Buren's Fabulous Chocolate Cake with Fluffy White Frosting.

There are more than 80 recipes in all, complete with photographs and personal biographies of their celebrity creators.

So run, don't walk, to buy this cookbook. Give copies to your friends and family. Enjoy the celebrity profiles and try their delicious recipes. Above all, remember that with a dream and a lot of hard work, anything can happen. The proof is in *The Jewish Celebrity Cookbook!*

Steven Raichlen

Steven Raichlen

Steven Raichlen is the author of *Healthy Jewish Cooking* (Viking) and *The Barbecue Bible* (Workman). His recipe for Sweet Potato Latkes appears on page 99.

Gloria Steinem
John E. Spero
Ellen Davis
Jane E. Brody
Joseph Lieberman
Abigail Van Buren
Beverly Sills
Judy Blume
Jeffrey Bishop
Dean Ornish
Art Spiegelman
Rabbi Marc Gellman
Herb Kohl
Bobby Hatfield
Andrew Weil
Joan Zakon Borysenko
Jerry Mander
Edward Koch
Don Rickles
Michael Feldman
Joel Siegel
Ben Sidran
Paul Newman
Rick Moranis
Donalee Patinkin Rubin
Beverly Sills
Barbara Barrie
Wendy Wasserstein
Joseph Heller
Arlen Specter
Mandy Patinkin
Robert Klein
Billy Joel
Steven Spielberg
Edward Asner
Steven Peterman
Al Clark
Faye Kellerman
Jon Voigt
Mollie Katzen
Nora Ephron
Barbara Walters
Susan Isaacs
Edward Koch
Wendy Selig-Prieb
David Zucker
Russel Feingold
Tana Hoban
Ben & Jerry
Henry Winkler
Claudia Cohen
Florence Eiseman
Steven Reichler
Susan Stamberg
Betty Comden
Dana Goldstein
Alfred Uhry
Ruth Pravda
David A. Adler
Roberta Peters
Marjorie Bialik
Ellen Bravo
Bernie Siegel
Charlotte Rae
Beatty Rutman
Theodore Bikel
Max Frankel
Tom Lantos
Marc Podwal
David H. Levy
Tana Hoban
Itzhak Perlman
Don Rickles
Joan Nathan
Robert Pinsky
Susan Estrich
Herb Kohl
Elaine Konigsburg
Roberta Peters
Shecky Greene
Aaron Sorkin
Charlotte Zucker
Theodore Bikel
John E. Spero
Abigail Van Buren
Beverly Sills
Judy Blume
Dean Ornish
Rabbi Marc Gellman
Robert Klein
Andrew Weil
Joan Zakon Borysenko
Don Rickles
Edward Asner
Mollie Katzen
Michael Feldman
Joel Siegel
Ben Sidran
Rick Moranis
Barbara Barrie
Steven Spielberg

Contents

Starters

Very Fattening Chopped Chicken Livers – **Itzhak Perlman** . . . 3
Old Father Robert's Fat Free Bean Dip – **Robert Pinsky** . . . 5
Hot Cream Cheese Hors d'Oeuvres – **Mandy Patinkin and Doralee Patinkin Rubin** . . . 7
Mimi Bochco's Gefilte Fish – **Charlotte Rae** . . . 9
Gefilte Fish–Indian Style – **Ruth Prawer Jhabvala** . . . 11
Traditional Passover Haroset – **Aaron Sorkin** . . . 13
Honey Whole Wheat Challah – **Rabbi Marc Gellman** . . . 14
Sweet-and-Sour Meatballs – **Jeffrey Bleustein** . . . 17
Grandma Bessie's Cabbage Borscht – **Shecky Greene** . . . 19
Grandma Dorothy's Better Cabbage Soup – **Susan Estrich** . . . 21
Kapusniak – **Art Spiegelman** . . . 23
Amy Richards' Carrot Soup – **Gloria Steinem** . . . 25
Grandma Dorothy's Chicken Soup – **Mark Podwal** . . . 27
Summer Gazpacho – **Edward Koch** . . . 29
Judy Sidran's Lentil Soup – **Ben Sidran** . . . 31
Mushroom Barley Soup – **Andrew Weil** . . . 33
Mom's "Just Like Out of a Can" Spinach Borscht – **Michael Feldman** . . . 36
Reservations – **Judy Sheindlin (Judge Judy)** . . . 37

Main Dishes

Dilled Fillets of Scrod with Joanne's Hollandaise Sauce – **Paul Newman** . . . 41
Barbara Freer Skibell's Succulent Blackened Shabbos Salmon – **Joseph Skibell** . . . 43
Grilled Tuna and Marinated Cucumber Salad – **Billy Joel** . . . 45
Port Clyde Broccoli Salad Sandwich – **Judy Blume** . . . 47
Skinless Baked Chicken – **Al Clark** . . . 49
Wisconsin Marinated Chicken – **Herb Kohl** . . . 51
Rina Lazarus' Salsa Chicken – **Faye Kellerman** . . . 53
Vegetarian Chili – **Dean Ornish** . . . 55
Leah Adler's Cheese Blintzes – **Steven Spielberg** . . . 57
"Dutch Babies" Pancake – **Beverly Sills** . . . 59
Matzah Brei for the Other 357 Days – **Rick Moranis** . . . 61
White Lasagna for Passover – **Don Rickles** . . . 63
Homemade Macaroni and Cheese Supreme – **Steven Peterman** . . . 66
Tuna Sandwich – **Wendy Wasserstein** . . . 67
Spaghetti Casserole – **Jerry Markbreit** . . . 69
Spaghetti with Sand – **Nora Ephron** . . . 71

Brunswick Stew – **Alfred Uhry** 73
Mother's Stuffed Cabbage Rolls – **Barbara Walters** 75
Sweet-and-Sour Stuffed Cabbage – **Jane E. Brody** 77
Mexican Meat Mixture – **David H. Levy** 79
Osso Buco – **Leon Uris** 81
Pot Roast – **Jim Abrahams** 83
Fresh Tongue and Sauce – **David Zucker** 85
Mexican Salad – **Henry Winkler** 87
Warm Spring Salad – **Ellen Taus** 89
The Perfect Hot Dog – **Jerry Reinsdorf** 91

Side Dishes

Balsamic Roasted New Potatoes – **Edward Asner** 95
Trio of Roasted Potatoes – **Anita Diamant** 97
Sweet Potato Latkes – **Steven Raichlen** 99
Sweet Potato Matzah Ball Tzimmes with Apricot Sauce – **Mayim Bialik** 101
Hungarian Potatoes – **Robert Klein** 103
Potato Pancake – **Darra Goldstein** 105
Potato Kugel – **Joey Bishop** 107
Tante Malka's Potato Kugel Deluxe – **Mollie Katzen** 109
Potato Zucchini Kugel – **Jesse Levis** 111
Daisy's Kugel – **Betty Aberlin** 113
Lokchen Kugel – **Elaine Konigsburg** 115
Mama Stamberg's Cranberry Relish – **Susan Stamberg** 117
Plum Compote – **Charlotte Zucker** 119
Senator and Mrs. Lieberman's Pistachio Rice Pilaf – **Joseph Lieberman** 121
Dorf's Kosher Risotto – **Michael Dorf** 123
Fried Green Beans with Coconut – **Barbara Barrie** 125
Brussels Sprouts with Maple-Orange-Walnut Butter – **Matt Lauer** 127
Kookoo Sabzi – **Letty Cottin Pogrebin** 129

Desserts

Fabulous Chocolate Cake and Fluffy White Frosting – **Abigail Van Buren (Dear Abby)** 133
Flourless Chocolate Cake – **Francine Klagsbrun** 135
Mrs. Finkelstein's Passover Chocolate Torte – **Joan Zakon Borysenko** 137
German Bundt Cake – **Tana Hoban** 139
Banana Chocolate Chip Loaf – **Beatty Rutman** 140
Chocolate Chip Cookie Dough Ice Cream and
Giant Chocolate Chip Cookies – **Ben Cohen and Jerry Greenfield** 142
Hannah's Cheesecake – **Russell D. Feingold** 145

Annette Lantos' Hungarian Rhapsody Dessert – **Tom Lantos** 147
Apple Crisp – **Theodore Bikel** 149
Blueberry Kuchen – **Johanna Hurwitz** 151
Blueberry Kuchen – **Florence Eiseman** 153
Joan Specter's Caramel Pineapple Cake Roll – **Arlen Specter** 155
Fruit Cobbler – **Joel Siegel** 157
Aunt Joan's Summer Connecticut Fruit Pie – **Joan E. Spero** 159
Mom's Sponge Cake – **Max Frankel** 161
Amandines – **Claudia Roden** 163
Brownies – **Ellen Bravo** 165
Aunt Lisl's Butter Cookies – **Joan Nathan** 167
Lemon Squares – **Wendy Selig-Prieb** 169
Mama's Mandelbrot – **Jane Breskin Zalben** 171
Aunt Sara's Mandelbrodt – **Susan Isaacs** 173
Moon Crescent Cookies – **David A. Adler** 175
Toffee Cookies – **Roberta Peters** 177
Life Pudding – **Bernie Siegel** 179

Index 181

Beverly Sills
Dean Ornish
Andrew Weil
Judy Blume
Herb Kohl
Edward Koch
Ben Sidran
Michael Feldman
Don Rickles
Joel Siegel
Rick Moranis
Barbara Barrie
Paul Newman
Steven Spielberg
Billy Joel
Al Clark
Steven Peterman
Faye Kellerman
Nora Ephron
Susan Isaacs
Mollie Katzen
Barbara Walters
David Zucker
Russel Feingold
Tana Hoban
Ben & Jerry
Henry Winkler
Florence Eisman
Susan Stamberg
Joan Nathan
Roberta Peters
Theodore Bikel
Bernie Siegel
Charlotte Rae
Itzhak Perlman
Robert Pinsky
Susan Estrich
Shecky Greene
Aaron Sorkin
Jim Abrahams
Joseph Lieberman
Jane E. Brody
Charlotte Zucker
Abigail VanBuren
Joan E. Spero
Art Spiegelman
Joan Zakon Borysenko
Rabbi Marc Gellman
Robert Klein
Edward Asner
Wendy Wasserstein
Arlen Specter
Mandy Patinkin
David A. Adler
Ruth Prawer Jhabvala
Anita Diamant
David H. Levy

Starters

Itzhak Perlman

Photo: Jonathan Levine

World-renowned concert violinist Itzhak Perlman was born in Tel Aviv, Israel. He studied at the Julliard School of Music and made his professional debut in 1963, at age eighteen, at Carnegie Hall. Perlman went on to win the Levintritt Competition in 1964 and has performed with major orchestras around the globe. He is known for his rich tone, technical mastery, and the joy he communicates in his playing. His musical talent has been described as "utterly limitless" by his colleague, Isaac Stern.

Very Fattening Chopped Chicken Livers

1 pound chicken fat
1 pound chicken livers, rinsed
1 medium onion, chopped fine
3 hard-boiled eggs, chopped
Salt to taste

1. Render chicken fat.*
2. Add chicken livers to rendered fat, turn off heat. Let the livers stew in the hot fat for 6 minutes.
3. Add chopped onion to livers and cook over medium heat until onions are slightly browned and livers are done.
4. Remove livers. In a very fine colander, let the fat drain—but not too much!
5. Chop liver with hard-boiled eggs. Add onion and salt.
6. Serve either with matzah or rye bread.

If you want more tang, add chopped raw onions (that's the way my mother used to make it). Make sure you have plenty of antacids—but it's worth it!

**Editor's note: Render chicken fat as follows:*

Place fat and ¼ cup cool water into a 2- to 3-quart saucepan. Cover pan and cook over medium heat until most of the fat is melted (about 20 minutes). Uncover and continue cooking until water evaporates, fat is golden, and solid pieces (also known as *gribeness* or cracklings) are browned. Drain and remove solid pieces. Pieces may be discarded or sprinkled with salt and nibbled.

Robert Pinsky

Boston University Photo Services

Robert Pinsky was poet laureate of the United States from 1997 to 2000. Appointed to this post by the Library of Congress, he instituted the "Favorite Poem Project," collecting recordings of Americans from all walks of life reading their favorite poems. Born in New Jersey, he earned an undergraduate degree from Rutgers University and a doctorate from Stanford University. Pinsky has published several books including *The Sounds of Poetry* and *The Figured Wheel: New and Collected Poems 1966-1996*, which was nominated for a Pulitzer Prize. He reads poetry regularly on PBS' *The News Hour With Jim Lehrer* and is poetry editor of *Slate*, an online magazine. Pinsky teaches in the graduate writing program at Boston University.

"To my wife and children it is a well-known fact and source of comedy that I do not cook. In this, oddly enough, I resemble my mother before me. When I was a child, we mostly ate take-out or, more often, food my grandmother prepared and sent over in Pyrex casseroles, jars, etc. She and her daughter, my mother, managed to argue about this arrangement more or less constantly.

So I was raised to think of food as more trouble than it is worth, and this recipe is in a way a joke about that fact. But the bean dip tastes very good and is indeed without fat. I recommend it."

– Robert Pinsky

Old Father Robert's
Fat Free Bean Dip!!!

3 16-ounce cans black beans
6 fresh limes (about 5 tablespoons lime juice)
Ground cumin to taste
3 or 4 cloves garlic, chopped

Take 3 cans of black beans. Drain the liquid by holding them in your fist over the sink.
Put beans in food processor.

Add the juice of 6 fresh limes, a lot of ground cumin, and 3 or 4 cloves of garlic, squoze and chopped and squished into the mix.
Turn that sucker on! (Put on lid first.)
Glop into bowl and eat with blue corn chips.

Serves one!

Mandy Patinkin and Doralee Patinkin Rubin

Multi-talented actor and singer Mandy Patinkin has appeared in theater, film and television. He won a Tony in 1980 for best actor in a musical for his portrayal of Che Guevara in *Evita*. In 1998, his one-man show, *Mamaloshen* (Yiddish for "mother tongue"), debuted on Broadway. Accompanied by piano and violin, Patinkin performed such Yiddish classics as "Belz" and "Raisins and Almonds" as well as Yiddish versions of "Take Me Out to the Ball Game" and "God Bless America." He credits the late Joseph Papp, founder of the New York Shakespeare Festival, for encouraging him to learn Yiddish songs. Patinkin starred in the movie *Yentl* and had a leading role on television's hospital drama *Chicago Hope*, which earned him an Emmy in 1995. He was born in Chicago and attended the University of Kansas and the Julliard School of Drama. Patinkin lives in New York City with his wife, actress and writer Kathryn Grody, and their two sons.

His mother, Doralee Patinkin Rubin, is the grandmother of fourteen. She lives in San Diego and has written several books, including *Grandma Doralee Patinkin's Jewish Family Cookbook*.

"This was Mandy's absolute favorite as a young child. At family dinner parties, we had to be sure he left some for the others. As my children grew older, I used a full slice of bread and served this to them for lunch. My grandchildren now clamor for this appetizer, as did their parents."

– *Doralee Patinkin Rubin*

Hot Cream Cheese Hors d'Oeuvres

1 3-ounce package cream cheese
½ teaspoon baking powder
1 egg yolk
1½ teaspoons grated onion, or to taste
Dash of salt
Paprika
12 rounds of white bread (6 slices)

1. Mix all of the ingredients together, except the paprika and bread.
2. Cut rounds from fresh white bread and toast just lightly on one side.
3. Spread cheese mixture on top, sprinkle with paprika, and, just before serving, broil until puffed and brown (watch carefully).

Makes 12 rounds.

Charlotte Rae

Actress Charlotte Rae is best known for her starring role as Mrs. Garrett on the popular television comedy *The Facts of Life,* which aired from 1979 to 1986. A graduate of Northwestern University's School of Drama, she went on to perform in the theater and on television. Her television appearances include roles on the *Phil Silvers Show; Car 54, Where are You?;* and *Diff'rent Strokes.*

"I think for your Milwaukee Jewish Day School's celebrity cookbook, the best recipe I could give you is my friend Mimi Bochco's recipe for gefilte fish. Her gefilte fish is perfection! Incidentally, she is the proud mother of Steven Bochco, the creator of *Hill Street Blues*, *L.A. Law*, and *NYPD Blue*.

I was born and raised in Milwaukee and love my friends, family, and hometown very much."

– *Charlotte Rae*

Mimi Bochco's Gefilte Fish *(not kosher for Passover)*

3 slices white bread, crusts removed
1¾ pounds whitefish, ground
1¾ pounds yellow pike, ground
½ pound carp, ground
3 large onions, 2 grated and 1 sliced
3 large eggs
Heads and bones of 3 fish, preferably whitefish, pike, and carp
2 teaspoons salt
⅛ teaspoon saffron threads, for color (optional)
½ teaspoon freshly ground black pepper
Horseradish, for serving

1. Soak bread in cold water to cover.
2. In a wooden bowl, combine the ground fish and grated onions. Mix with eggs.
3. Drain bread and add to mixture. Chop mixture until fish gets fluffy and pasty and sticks to the chopper, 20 to 30 minutes. This makes the fish light and airy.
4. Put fish heads and bones in a large pot. Place sliced onion on top, cover with cold water, and add 1 teaspoon of salt.
5. Gently shape fish mixture into egg-shaped dumplings, each about 3 by 2 inches. Put the gefilte fish in the pot on top of the onions, bring the water to a boil, reduce heat, and partially cover the pot.
6. Simmer very slowly for 2 hours.
7. Dissolve saffron in a little hot water and add to the pot for color, if desired, as the fish may have a slightly gray color without it.
8. Remove pot from heat and let cool for 10 to 15 minutes. Transfer the gefilte fish to a platter or deep dish.
9. Strain the cooking liquid, discard the solids, add pepper and remaining salt, and pour liquid over the fish.
10. Refrigerate to chill (the liquid will gel). Serve cold with plenty of horseradish.

Makes about 2 dozen. Enjoy!!!

Ruth Prawer Jhabvala

Photo: Merchant Ivory Productions

Writer Ruth Prawer Jhabvala is the winner of Academy Awards for Best Adapted Screenplay for both *A Room With a View* (1986) and *Howard's End* (1992). Her original screenplays include *Jefferson in Paris*. She was born in Germany and fled with her family to England in 1939 to escape the Nazis. While earning a master's degree in English literature from London University, she met architect Cyrus Jhabvala. They married and moved to India in 1951. There they raised three daughters, and Jhabvala wrote several novels and short story collections about life in India. Her 1975 novel *Heat and Dust* was the winner of Britain's prestigious Booker Award. It also marked the beginning of her long collaboration with Merchant Ivory Productions when the book was made into a film for which she wrote the screenplay. Jhabvala and her husband currently reside in New York.

"During my many years in India, I often longed for gefilte fish. However, I knew that for Indian taste it had to be spicier than what was served in my grandmother's house. So I devised this recipe, which I taught to my Indian cook. His name was Abdul—which possibly made him one of very few Abduls in the world who knew how to cook gefilte fish."

– ***Ruth Prawer Jhabvala***

Gefilte Fish–Indian Style

Fish

3 pounds assorted firm-fleshed white fish (such as 1 pound each carp, cod, and whitefish). Remove heads, skin, and bones; save heads and bones for broth.
2 eggs
½ cup cold water
3 tablespoons whole wheat flour
1 teaspoon ground cumin
1 teaspoon ground nutmeg
1 tablespoon ground coriander
1 hot green chili, finely chopped
½ teaspoon chili powder

Broth

Fish heads and bones
Salt and pepper
A piece of fresh ginger, peeled and chopped
5 cloves garlic, peeled and chopped
2 onions
3 carrots

1. Grind filleted fish, and add eggs, water, flour, and spices. Chill and shape into balls.

2. Combine fish heads and bones and remaining broth ingredients. Cover with water and bring to a boil.

3. Add prepared fish balls to boiling broth, turn heat to low, and simmer for 1 hour. Dot slices of carrot on fish balls.

Aaron Sorkin

Wunderkind Aaron Sorkin is creator, executive producer, and writer of two critically acclaimed television shows, *Sports Night* and *The West Wing* (winner of a Peabody Award for excellence in television). Raised in Scarsdale, New York, he graduated from Syracuse University in 1983 with a B.F.A. in theater. While in his twenties, he wrote the Broadway hit *A Few Good Men*, for which he received the Outer Critics Circle Award as Outstanding American Playwright. His screen adaptation of the play earned him Oscar nominations for best screenplay and best picture. Sorkin's screenwriting credits also include *The American President* and *Malice*. He lives in New York and Los Angeles with his wife, Julia.

"Aaron's response to the invitation to participate in this Jewish celebrity cookbook was a sense of pride and a wave of dismay: pride to be included in such illustrious company and have the opportunity to contribute to such a worthy cause, and dismay at the fact that, with a Broadway musical, thirteen episodes of a television series, and a movie for Warren Beatty to write, he'd be unable to give the project his full and proper attention. Given the circumstances, he asked me, wife of the Jewish celebrity, to give it a whack.

This spring we were invited to a Passover seder where each family was asked to bring a dish. Many of those invited are accomplished gourmands. Thus, it was with some trepidation I learned that Aaron had volunteered to bring the haroset.

The highlights of Aaron's culinary repertoire include Domino's pizza, McDonald's and well-done steak. However, he was quite confident and excited about preparing his dish. He made an explicit shopping list: apples, chopped walnuts, honey, and Manischewitz, and was very particular about the utensils he required: a knife and a bowl. When I suggested maybe a twist on the basic recipe—some dates and golden raisins? a food processor?—he responded quite seriously that there were some traditions not to be questioned.

It seems that when Aaron was twelve years old his parents became vegetarians. From then on, the traditional turkey and brisket were replaced by the celebratory salmon, with all the side dishes altered accordingly. Desperate to insure the salvation of at least part of the meal he so loved and looked forward to, Aaron proclaimed himself the maker of the haroset. And apples, walnuts, honey, and Manischewitz it would stay.

You've heard the expression 'make new friends but keep the old...'? Well, here is Aaron's rendition of our old friend, the Traditional Passover Haroset."

– Julia Sorkin

Traditional Passover Haroset

4 to 5 medium apples, peeled, cored, and chopped
¾ cup chopped walnuts
Honey
Ground cinnamon (Okay, so I convinced him this wasn't breaking the tradition.)
Manischewitz wine (or some other sweet red wine)

Combine chopped apples and walnuts, adjusting proportions to your liking. Add honey, cinnamon, and wine to taste.

Rabbi Marc Gellman

Rabbi Marc Gellman is the spiritual leader of Temple Beth Torah in Melville, New York, and president of the New York Board of Rabbis. He is best known for being a member of the "God Squad" (with Father Thomas Hartman) on ABC's *Good Morning America*. Together they offer commentary on religious issues. Gellman was born and raised in Milwaukee and received his undergraduate degree from the University of Wisconsin. Ordained at Hebrew Union College, he holds a Ph.D. from Northwestern University. He and his wife, Betty, are the parents of two children.

"My best friend is a priest. We went together to the Rosary Society and in appreciation received a 'Jesus Loves You' potholder, which I used to take the challah out of the oven. Is this a great country, or what!"

– ***Rabbi Marc Gellman***

Honey Whole Wheat Challah (Egg Bread)

via Levi and Nami Kelman

Bread

2 cups warm water (115°), divided
2 tablespoons brown sugar
2 cakes fresh yeast, or 6 packets dry yeast, or 4 tablespoons plus 1½ teaspoons bulk yeast
3 cups bread flour
3 cups whole wheat flour
3 cups additional bread or whole wheat flour, as needed
2 tablespoons kosher salt
⅓ cup peanut oil or other vegetable oil
3 extra-large eggs, beaten
½ cup honey
Raisins (optional)
Uncooked oatmeal or cornmeal, for baking sheet

Egg Wash

1 egg, beaten
1 tablespoon water
1 tablespoon honey
Sesame or poppy seeds (optional)

1. **For bread:** In medium bowl mix 1 cup warm water, brown sugar, and yeast. Wait until yeast forms thick, bubbling froth in bowl.
2. Mix 3 cups bread flour and 3 cups whole wheat flour together in mixing bowl or in bowl of a heavy-duty mixer or food processor with bread attachment. Make a well in the center of the bowl. Pour yeast mixture into the well and sprinkle salt on top. Mix to blend.
3. In another bowl mix remaining cup warm water, beaten eggs, oil, and honey. Add to flour mixture and blend well.
4. Knead dough, adding more flour (may be as much as 3 more cups) as mixture is being kneaded. The dough should be tacky but not gooey and should not stick to the board or, if kneaded in food processor or mixer, to the sides of the bowl.
5. After kneading dough thoroughly, turn dough into lightly oiled, warm bowl and cover with a towel. Let rise for 2½ hours or until doubled in volume.
6. Punch down dough and divide into the number of loaves you want (makes 2 large or 3 small loaves). (Important spiritual note: Pinch off a piece of dough about the size of an olive. This piece is to be thrown into the preheated oven after saying the following blessing: *Baruch ata adonai eloheinu melech ha'olam asher kidshanu b'mitzvotav vitzivanu l'hafrish chalah.*)*
7. For each challah, form dough into 3 ropes that are thicker in the middle and quite thin at the ends. Work raisins into each braid if you are including them. Braid by crossing first the right and then the left rope over the middle.
8. Sprinkle oats or cornmeal liberally on a cookie sheet and place each formed challah on top of bed of oats or cornmeal. Cover with a towel and let rise for at least another hour until doubled in volume again (if the yeast seems to be giving out, bake right away).
9. Fifteen minutes before baking, preheat oven to 350°F.
10. **For egg wash:** Mix beaten egg, honey, and water, and brush over each risen challah. Sprinkle with sesame or poppy seeds.
11. Bake in preheated oven for approximately 45 minutes or until bottom of bread sounds hollow when tapped with knuckles.

Shabbat shalom!! (Good sabbath, sabbath peace.)

Makes 2 large or 3 small loaves.

**Editor's note: This refers to the Biblical commandment to the children of Israel to set aside a small portion of dough (called "taking challah") from their bread baking for the sustenance of the Temple Priests. After the destruction of the Second Temple, it became customary to burn the piece of dough.*

Jeffrey Bleustein

Photo: Richard Brodzeller

Jeffrey Bleustein is chairman of the board, chief executive officer, and president of Harley-Davidson, Inc., the popular Milwaukee-based American motorcycle company. Prior to these responsibilities, Bleustein was executive vice-president, then president and chief operating officer of Harley-Davidson Motor Company. With an undergraduate degree in mechanical engineering from Cornell University and both an M.S. and Ph.D. in engineering mechanics from Columbia University, Bleustein's engineering leadership in the late '70s and early '80s significantly revitalized and expanded the Harley-Davidson product line.

"When my mother made these meatballs for her guests, she always had to double the recipe. It seems as if my sisters and I couldn't resist some preliminary tasting!"

– Jeffrey Bleustein

Sweet-and-Sour Meatballs

Sauce
1 16-ounce can jellied cranberry sauce
1 8- to 10-ounce can spaghetti meat sauce

Meatballs
1½ pounds lean, chopped chuck
½ cup bread crumbs
1 small onion, grated fine
1 egg
Salt and pepper

1. **For sauce:** Pour cranberry sauce and spaghetti sauce into deep skillet. Rinse sauce cans with ¾ cup water and add to skillet. Warm over low heat until cranberry sauce is melted, stirring occasionally.
2. **For meat:** Combine meat, bread crumbs, onion, ¼ cup water (or a little more), egg, and salt and pepper to taste. Mix well and shape into ¾-inch balls.
3. Add to warmed sauce and cook for 1½ hours, uncovered. Shake pot occasionally so sauce won't stick.

Can be made in advance and frozen.
To reheat, place in 325°F oven for about ½ hour.

Serves 4 to 6.

Shecky Greene

Comedian Shecky Greene has kept audiences laughing since he began his career while in college. Born in Chicago, Greene has entertained throughout the United States and overseas. A Las Vegas headliner for over thirty years, he appeared on the same bill as Elvis Presley on the night that Elvis made his Las Vegas debut at the Frontier Hotel in 1956. Greene has acted in many films, including *The Love Machine* and *Tony Rome*. His television credits include appearances on *Laverne and Shirley* and *Mad About You*. Greene and his wife, Marie, live in Los Angeles. They have two daughters.

"My mother was an excellent cook. She made great dishes like potato pancakes, veal chops, chicken soup, and matzah balls. But when she made her famous cabbage soup, I always wanted her to make an extra-big pot so it would last the whole week.

My wife, Marie, has captured the magic of my mother's recipe, and every time she makes it, I feel my mother, Bess, is in the kitchen with me.

Foods we had as children bring back great memories. I hope people who read this recipe and make this borscht feel some of the wonderful Jewish memories this soup has brought me."

– ***Shecky Greene***

Grandma Bessie's Cabbage Borscht

2 to 2½ pounds chuck roast with bone
2 quarts (8 cups) water
2 onions, chopped
2 cups canned whole tomatoes with juice
1 10½-ounce can tomato soup
3 pounds green cabbage, coarsely shredded
2 teaspoons salt, or to taste
½ teaspoon pepper
¼ cup lemon juice
2 tablespoons brown sugar
Horseradish, for serving

1. Combine meat and water in large soup pot. Bring to a boil and skim.
2. Add onions, tomatoes, and tomato soup. Cover and cook over low heat for 1 hour.
3. Add cabbage, salt, and pepper, and cook another hour.
4. Stir in lemon juice and brown sugar, and cook for 20 minutes.
5. Taste and adjust seasoning (salt, pepper, or sugar) if necessary.
6. Serve meat in soup or separately with horseradish.

Susan Estrich

Photo: Greg Lavy

Lawyer and educator Susan Estrich was the first woman editor of the *Harvard Law Review*. After graduating from Harvard Law School, one of her first jobs was clerking for Supreme Court Justice John Paul Stevens. She went on to become a tenured professor at Harvard Law School and the first woman to run a presidential campaign (for Michael Dukakis). The author of three books about the criminal justice system, she is a leading legal scholar on sexual assault law. Estrich is currently a professor of law and political science at the University of Southern California, a nationally syndicated newspaper columnist, and a regular television commentator on legal affairs. She lives in Los Angeles with her husband and their two children.

Grandma Dorothy's Better Cabbage Soup

1 large Vidalia onion, sliced
1 tablespoon canola oil
1 head green cabbage, shredded
Kosher salt
1 28-ounce can crushed or whole tomatoes, with juice
8 cups water
1 teaspoon salt
½ teaspoon white pepper
2 to 3 tablespoons lemon juice (approximately 1 lemon)
2 to 3 tablespoons sugar (same amount as lemon juice)
Raisins
Nonfat yogurt or sour cream (optional)

1. Place cabbage in a colander and sprinkle with kosher salt.
2. Sauté onion in oil over medium heat in a large soup pot. Rinse cabbage well and drain. When onion just begins to brown, add cabbage to pot. Reduce heat to low. Let it steam, covered, for 20 to 30 minutes, stirring occasionally from the bottom of the pot, until cabbage is soft. Add a little water if cabbage begins to stick.
3. Add tomatoes and juice, water, salt, pepper, lemon juice, and sugar. Toss in a handful of raisins. Bring to a boil, then lower flame and simmer for about 2 hours.
4. Serve with a dollop of nonfat yogurt or sour cream. The soup tastes even better the next day.

Makes about 4½ quarts.

Susan's note: Raisins! Raisins! Buy a little teeny box if you can't control yourself with an open family-size box around the house. And remember, Grandma Dorothy had small hands. And, of course, if you want to stay away from sugar, you may sweeten the soup with artificial sweetener when it's done. You may also substitute vegetable-oil cooking spray for the canola oil.

Art Spiegelman

Photo: Bob Adelman

Born in Stockholm, Sweden, author and cartoonist Art Spiegelman grew up in Queens, New York. He is the author/illustrator of *Maus: A Survivor's Tale* (1986) and *Maus II* (1992), which received National Book Critic's Circle nominations and a Pulitzer Prize. These books detail his parents' experiences during the Holocaust. Spiegelman worked for Topps Gum Co. from 1966 to 1988 creating novelty cards, stickers, and candy products. He co-founded *RAW* magazine with his wife, Francoise Mouly, in 1980. His work has been exhibited in the U.S. and abroad, including a show at the Museum of Modern Art in New York. Spiegelman is currently a consulting editor to *The New Yorker* and lives in Manhattan with his wife and their two children.

"Once I invited my high school pal, Jon Wong, for some of Mom's home cooking. It was February, and she served up my favorite winter dish, a hot, steamy, tangy kapusniak, a soup recipe from the Old Country that makes those Campbell's Hearty 'Man-Pleasers' seem like limp-wristed sissy-water by comparison.

Jon looked dubiously at the savory bowl and gingerly tried a tentative half-spoonful of the indescribable sweet-and-sour broth. His mouth puckered to a tiny asterisk as if he'd swallowed a live frog. For five minutes he made soft, quick panting sounds while the Spiegelman family happily slurped through several helpings. Jon finally found his voice and hoarsely whispered, 'I can't believe it—Jews eat SAUERKRAUT soup!'

He refused to try another drop, or even try the *chulent* stew that Mom made as the main dish. . . . I guess he thought it was made with dead babies.

ONCE I invited my high school pal, Jon Wong, for some of Mom's home cooking!"

– Art Spiegelman

Kapusniak

KAPUSNIAK- 6-8 servings

- 1 pound of sauerkraut, canned or fresh, the more sour the better.
- 2 pounds Flanken, or short ribs.
- ½ cup brown sugar.
- 2 crushed cloves of garlic
- 1 pound canned tomatoes
- 4 cups of water.

Place everything into a 5 quart kettle and simmer for 2-2½ hours, stirring frequently, until the meat is tender. Remove meat, then skim fat off soup. (If possible, refrigerate overnight, then remove congealed fat.)

Cut meat into bite-size pieces and replace into soup. Reheat and serve.

Gloria Steinem

Writer, editor, lecturer, and political activist Gloria Steinem co-founded *Ms.* magazine in 1972. Born in Toledo, Ohio, and a graduate of Smith College, she began her writing career as a political columnist for *New York* magazine in 1968. She is a founder of the National Women's Political Caucus and the author of several books; as a result of her accomplishments, she was named to the National Women's Hall of Fame. Steinem is a member of a feminist consortium that purchased *Ms.* magazine in 1998. She lives in New York and is a consulting editor for *Ms.*

"Thank you for your kind note to Gloria Steinem. Because Gloria only rarely cooks, she doesn't have a favorite recipe. Her cooking consists mostly of "Nile Spice" soups and take-out. Because Gloria and I are very good friends and she often eats my cooking, she asked me to share one of my favorite recipes—Carrot Soup. This is something that I often make for myself and for Gloria. So this comes from Gloria, but via me. I hope it still helps."

– Amy Richards

Amy Richards'
Carrot Soup

4 tablespoons sweet butter
2 cups yellow onions, chopped
12 large carrots (1½ to 2 pounds), peeled and chopped
4 cups chicken stock (or vegetable, if you prefer)
1 cup freshly squeezed orange juice (or apple juice, if you prefer)*
Salt and pepper to taste
Orange zest to sprinkle on top

**If you use apple juice, I recommend adding some freshly chopped ginger, too.*

1. Melt butter in a large pot. Add onions (and ginger, if using apple juice) and cover. Cook for approximately 25 minutes or until onions are lightly colored.
2. Add carrots and stock and bring to a boil. Reduce heat, cover, and simmer until carrots are tender, approximately 30 minutes.
3. Transfer solids and 1 cup of stock to a food processor. Process until smooth and return to pot.
4. Add 1 cup of freshly squeezed orange juice (or apple juice). Heat and serve. Garnish with salt and pepper and orange zest (if using orange juice).

Makes 2½ quarts.

Mark Podwal

Photo: Nancy Crampton

Mark Podwal is a dermatologist and artist whose works are owned by The Metropolitan Museum of Art, The Jewish Museum in New York, and The Israel Museum in Jerusalem. He has illustrated many books (several of which he has also written) including *King Solomon and His Magic Ring* (1999), Elie Wiesel's first book for children. His drawings have appeared on the op-ed page of *The New York Times,* and a Podwal painting graces the cover of *Live in the Fiddler's House*, Itzhak Perlman's klezmer CD. He lives with his wife and two sons in the New York City area.

"Several years ago, during a birthday party for my son Michael, my mother suffered an attack of severe abdominal pain. Not wanting to bother anyone with her problems, she kept her symptoms a secret. My mother had cooked her usual feast for the birthday celebration and was determined not to spoil the fun. The fact that, in addition to being an artist, I am also a physician apparently made no impression on her. Two days later, my mother called to say that she was being admitted to the hospital for gallbladder surgery.

On the eve of the scheduled gallbladder removal, my friend Simon visited my mother in the hospital. Simon had long been a great fan of my mother's chicken soup and wanted to make sure he had the recipe before the surgery. My mother survived the procedure and so did the recipe. However, she says she never cooks according to a recipe. Nevertheless, here is what my mother told Simon."

– Mark Podwal

Grandma Dorothy's Chicken Soup

1 3- to 4-pound chicken with skin on, cut into 8 pieces
8 chicken wings with skin on
3 small whole onions, with a cross cut into each one
1 bunch carrots (about 1 pound), peeled and halved, tops discarded
4 to 6 stalks celery, tied together
2 parsnips, peeled
4 to 5 cloves garlic
Salt to taste, at least 1 teaspoon
½ to 1 whole bunch of dill (3 to 4 sprigs or to taste)
10 pints water
Pepper, for serving

1. Combine all ingredients except pepper in an 8- to 12-quart pot.
2. Bring to a boil and skim off the foam.
3. Reduce to a simmer and cook for 2 to 2½ hours covered. Skim as needed.
4. Separate the soup from the solids and put soup into a container.
5. Put into the refrigerator and cool. Skim off the fat the next day.
6. Adjust salt to taste before serving.
7. Serve with pepper.

Editor's note: When soup is finished and chicken is cool enough to handle, it may be removed from bones, cut into bite-sized pieces, and returned to soup.

Edward Koch

Photo by Konstantin

A colorful and outspoken figure, Ed Koch was the mayor of New York City from 1977 to 1989. After leaving the mayor's office, he returned to the practice of law. The author of several books, including a memoir entitled *I'm Not Done Yet!: Keeping at It, Remaining Relevant, and Having the Time of My Life,* he appeared on the popular television show *The People's Court.* Koch is a co-founder of *TheLaw.com,* a legal Web site for consumers, which provides information on such topics as divorce and bankruptcy. He was born in the Bronx and attended N.Y.U. Law School.

Summer Gazpacho

The appeal of this gazpacho to me is its thickness and crunchiness.

3 ounces olive oil
3 ounces wine vinegar
Salt and pepper to taste (use Crazy Jane lemonade pepper if available)
1 large cucumber, chopped
2 green peppers, chopped
1 6- to 8-ounce can pimentos, chopped
3 large tomatoes, chopped
2 large onions (preferably white), chopped
3 garlic cloves, diced
1 32-ounce can tomato juice
Croutons, for serving

1. Combine all ingredients except tomato juice and croutons in blender or food processor. Process on lowest speed or pulse until coarsely ground.
2. Transfer to large container and add tomato juice. Stir to blend. Place in refrigerator for at least 2 hours.
3. Serve with croutons.

Serves 8 generously.

Ben Sidran

Jazz musician Ben Sidran can't remember a time when he didn't play the piano. Born and raised in Racine, Wisconsin, he attended the University of Wisconsin and received a Ph.D. in American Studies from the University of Sussex in England. After joining the Steve Miller band in London, and playing with such luminaries as Eric Clapton and Peter Frampton, he returned to the U.S. to write and record songs and tour with bands. He also produced jazz records and radio and television programs about jazz. When his son Leo turned five, Sidran began to reconnect with his Jewish roots. This led to the production of *Life's a Lesson*, an album of Jewish jazz musicians performing Hebrew liturgical music. Leo often accompanies his father on the drums.

"I won't lie—I don't cook. In part because my wife Judy is such a great cook and she really loves to prepare meals, my main role is hanging around the kitchen and kibitzing while she's cooking. And, of course, eating. I love her food, and in the winters I particularly love the soups she makes. They are delicious, and they seem to get even better after spending a day or two in the refrigerator. One of my favorites is her lentil soup, and she has been kind enough to let me borrow her recipe and pass it along to you."

– Ben Sidran

Judy Sidran's
Lentil Soup

1 pound lentils (about 2⅓ cups)
1 large onion, chopped (1½ to 2 cups)
2 to 3 cloves garlic, chopped
2 ribs celery, chopped
1 28-ounce can Italian plum tomatoes, chopped
1 large bay leaf
4 sprigs parsley
Mint, basil, oregano, and cumin to taste*
⅓ cup olive oil
Salt and freshly ground pepper to taste
2 tablespoons red wine vinegar
2 cups fresh spinach, chopped (optional)

1. Wash lentils and place in soup pot with warm water to cover, about 2 quarts. Let stand for 1 hour, then bring to a boil.
2. Add onion, garlic, celery, and tomatoes. Cover and simmer for 1 hour.
3. Stir in herbs, oil, and seasonings. Continue to simmer covered for 1½ hours, until thick and tender, stirring occasionally.
4. Add spinach and vinegar. Heat through, until spinach is thoroughly wilted.
5. Remove bay leaf before serving.
6. Serve with warm pita or crusty French bread. Freezes very well, and is great to have on hand.

Serves 10 as a first course, 5 as a meal.

**Editor's note: Our testers used a few fresh mint leaves, chopped, 1 tablespoon basil, 2 teaspoons oregano, and 1 teaspoon cumin.*

Andrew Weil

Photo: Lisa Law

A leading proponent of alternative medicine, Andrew Weil teaches alternative medicine, mind-body interactions, and medical botany at the College of Medicine, University of Arizona, where he founded the Program in Integrative Medicine. He received an A.B. in biology (botany) from Harvard and an M.D. from Harvard Medical School. He is the author of numerous books, including *8 Weeks to Optimal Health* and *Eating Well for Optimum Health*.

"Mushroom barley soup is a classic. I asked my friend Betty Anne Sarver to come up with a vegetarian version, which she did. If you use shiitake mushrooms, you will get the added benefit of their immune-enhancing and cholesterol-lowering properties. You can use vegetable broth powder or the great organic vegetable broth sold in cartons at natural food stores."

– Andrew Weil

Mushroom Barley Soup
from Betty Anne Sarver

1 cup quick-cooking pearl barley
3 tablespoons olive oil
1¼ cup onions, chopped
2 cloves garlic, chopped
1 pound mushrooms (shiitake, portobello, etc.), sliced
4 tablespoons dry sherry
8 cups vegetable stock, divided*
4 tablespoons shoyu (soy sauce)
2 teaspoons dried dill weed

1. In a 3-quart pot, cook barley in 2 cups stock until tender.
2. While barley simmers, sauté onions and garlic in oil until onions are translucent. Add sliced mushrooms and sherry, and cook uncovered until mushrooms are soft.
3. Add mushroom mixture, shoyu, remaining stock, and dill to barley.
4. Bring to boil, lower heat, and simmer covered for 20 to 30 minutes.

**Note:* If you wish to make your own stock: Wash 6 large organic potatoes and remove the peels in strips at least ¼-inch thick. Put the peels in a large pot (and save the potatoes for another use). To the pot add 1 large onion, sliced; 2 carrots, peeled and sliced; 1 small stalk celery, sliced; 1 sprig of parsley; and 1 clove garlic, chopped. Add 6 cups cold water, bring to a boil, cover, reduce heat, and simmer slowly for 1½ hours, adding water if necessary to keep the level constant. Strain.

Michael Feldman

Photo: Matthew Gilson

Dubbed "The King of Small Talk Radio" by *The Wall Street Journal,* Michael Feldman made his radio debut in 1965 when he earned an appearance on a Milwaukee radio program by winning an essay contest. After graduating from the University of Wisconsin, he taught for eight years, recalling, "It was an English class and we spoke it." Feldman began his critically acclaimed and highly popular radio call-in quiz show *Michael Feldman's Whad'ya Know* in 1985. It is now carried by over three hundred Public Radio International affiliates and has a weekly audience of 1.3 million fans. Feldman lives with his wife and two daughters in Madison, Wisconsin.

Judy Sheindlin

Photo: Sven Arnstein

Witty and outspoken, Judge Judy Sheindlin presides over real-life court cases on the courtroom television show *Judge Judy*. Raised in Brooklyn, she was appointed to a judgeship in Bronx family court in 1982. In 1986, she was promoted to supervising judge of the family court in Manhattan. A *60 Minutes* profile led to an offer of her own show, which debuted in 1996. Her books include *Don't Pee On My Leg and Tell Me It's Raining*, a critique of the family court system. Jerry Sheindlin, her husband of over twenty years, was a New York City Supreme Court judge, and is now the presiding judge on television's *The People's Court*. They have five children and live in Manhattan.

"Again I received your letter. As much as I would like to, it is difficult to help you with your request. According to my husband, I haven't cooked in twenty-two years—I am an expert in making reservations.

If you ever do a book on the art of reserving a table, please keep me in mind."

– Judy Sheindlin

Beverly Sills
Dean Ornish
Andrew Weil
Judy Blume
Judy Body
Herb Kohl
Betty Hadlin
Don Rickles
Rabbi Marc Gellman
Abigail Van Buren
Joan E. Spero
Art Spiegelman
Jeffrey Blankfein
Joan Zaken Borysenko
Jerry Minkelreit
Susan Estrich
Michael Feldman
Joel Siegel
Edward Koch
Ben Sidran
Paul Newman
Rick Moranis
Barbara Barrie
Donalee Patinkin Rubin
Mandy Patinkin
Wendy Wasserstein
Joseph Heller
Billy Joel
Steven Peterman
Al Clark
Steven Spielberg
Faye Kellerman
Jim Weiss
Susan Isaacs
Mollie Katzen
Robert Klein
Joey Bishop
Edward Asner
Nora Ephron
Jessie Davis
Barbara Walters
David Zucker
Wendy Seltzer-Prieb
Russel Feingold
Claudia Cohen
Steven Reichler
Matt Lauer
Tana Hoban
Ben & Jerry
Henry Winkler
Florence Eiseman
Letty Cottin Pogrebin
Dana Goldstein
Alfred Uhry
David A. Adler
Ruth Prawer Jhabvala
Anita Diamant
Susan Stamberg
Joan Nathan
Roberta Peters
Marjorie Bielik
Ellen Burstyn
Theodore Bikel
Bernie Siegel
Tom Lantos
Charlotte Rae
Marc Polonsky
Betty Putnam
Mort Frankel
Robert Pinsky
Itzhak Perlman
Davis H. Levy
Shelley Greene
Aaron Sorkin
Elaine Konigsburg
Johanna Hurwitz
Charlotte Zucker
Ellen Pauls
Jim Abraham
Joseph Lieberman
Jane E. Brody

Main Dishes

Paul Newman

Photo: Robert Norman

Paul Newman, president and founder of Newman's Own, Inc., is probably best known for his spectacularly successful food conglomerate. In addition to giving the profits to charity, he also ran Frank Sinatra out of the spaghetti sauce business. On the downside, the spaghetti sauce is outgrossing his films.

He graduated from Kenyon College "magna cum lager" and in the process begat a laundry business, which was the only student-run enterprise on Main Street. Yale University later awarded him an honorary doctorate of Humane Letters for unknown reasons.

He has won four Sports Car Club of America National Championships and is listed in the Guinness Book of World Records as the oldest driver (age seventy) to win a professionally sanctioned race (twenty-four hours of Daytona, 1995).

He is married to the best actress on the planet, was number 19 on Nixon's enemy list, and, purely by accident, has done fifty-one films and four Broadway plays.

He is generally considered by professionals to be the worst fisherman on the East Coast.

Dilled Fillets of Scrod à la Newman

Coming in a distant second to Joanne's Sole Cabernet is my own Dilled Fillet of Scrod, which I bake in the oven, liberally coating it with lots of fresh dill, butter, and lemon juice.

2 pounds scrod fillets
3 to 4 tablespoons chopped fresh dill or 1 tablespoon dried
½ cup (1 stick) unsalted butter, melted
¾ cup dry white wine
1 recipe Joanne's Hollandaise Sauce

1. Preheat oven to 375°F.
2. Wash fillets and pat dry with paper towels. Arrange in a single layer in a 13 x 9 x 2-inch baking dish.
3. Cover with dill.
4. Heat butter and wine together in a small saucepan until butter melts. Pour over fish.
5. Bake for 20 minutes, or just until fish separates easily when touched with a fork.
6. Serve with Joanne's Hollandaise Sauce

Serves 4.

Joanne's Hollandaise Sauce

3 egg yolks
3 tablespoons cold water
½ cup (1 stick) lightly salted butter, melted
Freshly ground pepper to taste
Juice of ½ lemon

1. Place egg yolks and water in the top of a double boiler over hot, but not boiling, water. Whisk rapidly until mixture thickens and an instant-read thermometer registers 160°F.
2. Remove from heat. Add butter, little by little, while continuing to whisk.
3. Add pepper.
4. Add lemon juice just before serving.

Makes 2 cups.

Joseph Skibell

Writer Joseph Skibell is best known for his holocaust novel, *A Blessing on the Moon*. A recipient of a James A. Michener Fellowship, he taught at the University of Wisconsin, where he was the 1996-1997 Halls Fellow in fiction. Skibell is Assistant Professor of English at Emory University.

"My wife, Barbara Freer Skibell, knows a lot about food. She knows as much about basil as Chagall did about blue. She knows exactly how long to cook individual vegetables, for instance. (Six minutes for broccoli, four minutes for snap peas, fifteen minutes for carrots, etc.) I have always joked that she is a 'food dreamer.' In a primitive village, the elders of the tribe would have told her, 'You go into your hut and dream. We will wait.'

I'm very lucky to live with her.

For Shabbos, she cooks an incredible dinner each week. A fresh leafy green salad with homemade dressing, homemade whole-grain challah, spiced cooked fresh vegetables, sometimes a pasta dish, and, although she's tried many different kinds of fish, she keeps returning to a succulent salmon.

'The great thing about this meal,' says Barbara, 'is that it works perfectly for Shabbos because the fish can sit for up to an hour and it only becomes more and more delicious. It also makes a wonderful spread when mixed with goat cheese for Third Meal.'"

– Joseph Skibell

Barbara Freer Skibell's

Succulent Blackened Shabbos Salmon

1. Preheat oven to at least 350°F for at least 30 minutes.* (This is a good time to roast your vegetables or bake your challah.)
2. Place one piece of filleted salmon (8 ounces to 3 pounds; leave the skin on one side) on a thick piece of aluminum foil. Turn up the sides of the foil in order to catch the juices.
3. Spread the side without skin with a generous layer of Patak's Curry Paste. (Use hot, mild, or medium, according to taste. Barbara uses hot for a nice, spicy meal. The paste is available in the specialty department of many grocery stores.)
4. Place the fish in the broiler with the skin side down and the sauce side up. Broil for 5 minutes.
5. Turn oven off. Allow fish to remain in oven for at least 15 minutes or until all the prayers and blessings at the table have been said. Leaving the fish in the broiler is crucial to give it an extremely moist butter-like texture. The paste creates a crusty, black coating that is delicious.

**Editor's note: If broiler is separate from oven, set controls to broil and preheat 15 minutes. Proceed with steps 2 through 4. Turn broiler off and transfer fish to warmed oven. Continue with step 5.*

Billy Joel

Photo: Len Irish

Before 1973, one might have encountered William Joseph Martin Joel playing the piano in a Los Angeles piano bar. Later encounters would be in much larger venues, as Bronx-born Billy Joel found a worldwide audience for his singing and songwriting. Raised in Levittown, New York, he began performing while still in high school. In 1973, Joel signed a contract with Columbia Records; his *Piano Man* album was released the same year. In 1977 *The Stranger* album went multi-platinum and propelled him to stardom. It won Grammys in 1978 for both record of the year and song of the year for "Just the Way You Are." Other classics composed and performed by Joel include "Uptown Girl" and "My Life." In recognition of his songwriting accomplishments, he was inducted into the Songwriters' Hall of Fame in 1992. Joel is currently devoting his talents to composing classical music. An avid sailor, he helped design a high-end speedboat called the Shelter Island Runabout, which has been sold since 1996.

Grilled Tuna and Marinated Cucumber Salad

This is one of my favorite recipes and should be started a day ahead of time.

FIRST DAY

Fish

Marinate fresh tuna steaks overnight in the refrigerator in a mixture consisting of:

4 parts olive oil
1 part teriyaki sauce
1 part lemon juice
Salt, pepper, and parsley

Make enough marinade to completely cover tuna steaks.

Cucumber Salad*

The cucumber salad should also be prepared and refrigerated a day ahead of time. Peel cucumbers and slice thin. Combine cucumbers with a mixture of:

White wine vinegar
Coriander
Salt
Pepper
A dash of olive oil

Note: Some people like to add chopped white onions. However, if your love interest is not sharing the salad with you, I recommend that you leave out the onions.

**Editor's note: For cucumber portion of the salad, our testers used (for each cucumber) ¼ cup vinegar and ½ teaspoon ground coriander.*

SECOND DAY

1. Grill the tuna steaks over a barbecue or open flame. Don't overcook the tuna; it should be pink on the inside.
2. After you have grilled the tuna steaks, break them into chunks and combine with the marinated, chilled cucumber mixture. However, before you mix the tuna and the cucumber, drain the cucumber salad and discard the liquid. Bon Appétit!

Judy Blume

Author Judy Blume is well-known for books that deal with the realities of young adolescents. Her many published works include *Are You There God? It's Me, Margaret* (selected as outstanding children's book of 1970); *Tales of a Fourth Grade Nothing;* and *Superfudge*. Her adult novels include *The New York Times* best-seller *Summer Sisters*, published in 1998. Her books have sold worldwide and have been translated into twenty languages. Blume grew up in Elizabeth, New Jersey, and received a bachelor's degree in education from New York University. She is the founder and trustee of The Kids Fund and a spokesperson for the National Coalition Against Censorship. She lives on islands up and down the East Coast with her husband, George Cooper, who writes nonfiction. They have three children and one grandchild.

"During the summer of 1980, I spent a month in Maine, on a small island off Port Clyde. Twice a week we grocery shopped by boat and always stopped for lunch at a tiny sandwich shop. That's where I first tasted broccoli salad. By the end of the month, I convinced the owner of the shop to tell me her secret, which I'm happy to share with you. It's delicious, healthy, and tastes a lot better than it sounds (as long as you like broccoli!). It can be made from fresh uncooked or lightly steamed broccoli."

– Judy Blume

Port Clyde Broccoli Salad Sandwich

1 cup broccoli, raw or lightly steamed
1 teaspoon (or less) mayonnaise
Juice from a lemon wedge
Salt and pepper to taste

Chop broccoli florets into tiny pieces. (I use a food processor.) Add just enough mayonnaise to keep the salad together. Squeeze in the juice from a wedge of lemon. Add salt and pepper to taste. Mix well. Spread on your favorite kind of bread. Yum!

Al Clark

An American League umpire since 1976, Al Clark was born in Trenton, New Jersey, and attended Eastern Kentucky University. After completing an umpire specialization course in 1972, Clark began his career in the Midwest League (Class A). He umpired at both the 1983 (Baltimore Orioles vs. Philadelphia Phillies) and 1989 (Oakland A's vs. San Francisco Giants) World Series as well as the 1984 and 1995 All-Star Games. Clark and his wife have one child and live in Virginia, where he enjoys gourmet cooking during the off-season.

"It is with pleasure that I participate in your fundraiser cookbook endeavor. Unfortunately, because of the Brewers' switch to the National League, I do not come to your great city any longer, although I have very fond memories of great people and friends from Milwaukee.

Thank you for thinking of me!"

– Al Clark

Skinless Baked Chicken

Chicken parts (legs, thighs, and breasts), skinned and washed in cool water
Olive oil
Garlic powder
Parsley
Oregano
Italian-style bread crumbs
Worcestershire sauce
Paprika

1. Preheat oven to between 350° and 375°F (any temperature within this range is fine).
2. Place all chicken parts on baking pan.
3. Sprinkle with olive oil, garlic powder, parsley, and oregano. Cover all with bread crumbs. Dab all with Worcestershire sauce. Sprinkle with paprika.
4. Bake 50 minutes to 1 hour, or until juices run clear when meat is pierced.
5. Serve and enjoy.

Herb Kohl

Born and raised in Milwaukee, Herb Kohl has represented Wisconsin in the U.S. Senate since 1988. After completing his undergraduate studies at the University of Wisconsin, he earned an MBA from Harvard University. He then helped build his family-owned business, Kohl's grocery and department stores. In 1985, Kohl bought the Milwaukee Bucks basketball team to insure that they remained in Milwaukee. He is active in Wisconsin charities, including the Herb Kohl Educational Foundation, which has awarded $1.8 million to Wisconsin students and teachers.

Wisconsin Marinated Chicken

½ cup water
¼ cup soy sauce
¼ cup orange or pineapple juice
2 tablespoons corn oil
½ cup brown sugar
½ teaspoon garlic powder
½ teaspoon ginger
1 or 2 chickens, cut in pieces

1. Preheat oven to 350°F.
2. Mix all ingredients except chicken. Stir until sugar dissolves.
3. Put chicken into 1 or 2 plastic bags. Pour marinade over chicken and marinate in refrigerator at least 3 hours.
4. Transfer chicken to a baking dish. Pour marinade over chicken. Cover pan and bake for 1½ hours, basting occasionally.

Faye Kellerman

Photo: Jonathan Exley

Writer Faye Kellerman is known for her extremely popular series of mystery novels featuring Peter Decker and Rina Lazarus, a Jewish detective and his wife. Kellerman was born in St. Louis and grew up in California, where she earned degrees in math and dentistry at UCLA. Her first novel, *The Ritual Bath*, was published in 1986. She is married to crime novelist Jonathan Kellerman and has four children.

"Although Rina and I keep the dietary laws of traditional Judaism, we still have room for creativity in the kitchen. Living in Los Angeles, we're influenced by regional cuisine as exemplified by Rina's Southwestern meal in *False Prophet*. Here is her personal recipe for Salsa Chicken. She might serve this entree with wild rice and a fresh avocado-and-grapefruit salad. Enjoy."

– Faye Kellerman

Rina Lazarus'
Salsa Chicken

Salsa
4 large tomatoes, coarsely chopped
1 small onion, finely chopped
1 small green pepper, seeded and diced
1 clove fresh garlic, minced
2 tablespoons fresh lemon juice
2 tablespoons minced fresh coriander (cilantro)
2 teaspoons minced fresh parsley
½ teaspoon salt
½ teaspoon pepper

Chicken
2 tablespoons flour
½ teaspoon garlic powder
½ teaspoon salt
½ teaspoon pepper
6 boneless chicken breasts (each ½ inch thick)
Oil for frying
Parsley sprigs and lemon slices for garnish

1. **For salsa:** In a medium bowl mix together tomatoes, onion, green pepper, garlic, lemon juice, coriander, parsley, salt, and pepper. Set aside in refrigerator for at least 2 hours.
2. Preheat oven to 350°F. Grease a shallow baking pan.
3. **For chicken:** In a separate bowl mix together flour, garlic powder, salt, and pepper.
4. Dredge chicken in the dry mixture.
5. Sauté chicken in oil until it turns slightly brown.
6. Place chicken in pan and bake for 30 minutes or until done to taste.
7. Remove chicken from oven and place on a serving platter.
8. Decorate with parsley sprigs and lemon slices. Serve hot with salsa on the side.

Serves 6.

Recipe from the paperback edition of False Prophet.

Dean Ornish

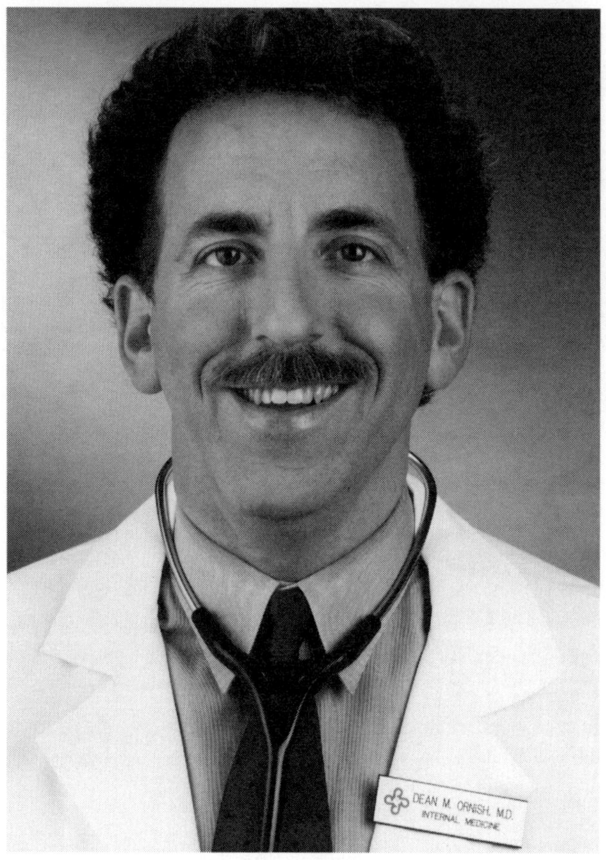

For over twenty years, Dean Ornish has directed clinical research demonstrating that comprehensive lifestyle changes in diet, exercise, smoking habits, and stress management may reverse coronary heart disease without drugs or surgery. His program also emphasizes the importance of emotional and spiritual well-being to heart health. A graduate of Baylor College of Medicine, he was a clinical fellow in medicine at Harvard Medical School. He holds the Buchsbaum Chair at the nonprofit Preventative Medicine Research Institute in Sausalito, California, which he founded in 1984. He is a clinical professor of medicine at the University of California, San Francisco.

"Vegetarian Chili is from *Eat More, Weigh Less* and is one of my favorites."

– ***Dean Ornish***

Vegetarian Chili
from Jean-Marc Fullsack

You can prepare and refrigerate this 2 to 3 days ahead of time. You can also freeze it for up to 3 months, although the corn may darken somewhat.

1 cup plus 2 tablespoons vegetable stock, divided
¾ cups diced carrots
1 cup diced onions
1 cup diced green bell peppers
1 cup diced red bell peppers
1 cup diced celery
1 tablespoon minced garlic
1 teaspoon dried oregano
1 teaspoon dried thyme
½ teaspoon ground coriander
1 teaspoon ground cumin
1½ teaspoons chili powder
4 ounces minced canned jalapeño peppers, or to taste
2 cups chopped tomatoes
3 cups cooked pinto beans
1 cup fresh corn kernels
1½ tablespoons red miso paste
1 tablespoon lemon juice
1 teaspoon red wine vinegar
1 teaspoon salt
Freshly ground black pepper
½ cup chopped fresh cilantro
Additional chopped cilantro for garnish

1. In a large, nonstick pan in 2 tablespoons vegetable stock "sweat"* the carrots, onions, green and red bell peppers, and celery for 4 to 5 minutes.
2. Add the garlic, oregano, thyme, coriander, cumin, chili powder, jalapeños, tomatoes, pinto beans, and remaining vegetable stock. Bring to a boil, reduce heat, and simmer for 20 minutes.
3. Add a little extra vegetable or bean liquid if a "saucier" chili is desired. Add corn kernels and simmer for 7 minutes.
4. In a small bowl combine the red miso, lemon juice, and vinegar until dissolved. Stir miso mixture into the chili with ½ cup cilantro.
5. Season to taste with salt and pepper. Serve hot with the additional chopped cilantro.

Makes 7 cups.

**Editor's note: To "sweat" vegetables, place them in the vegetable stock, cover, and cook over moderate heat.*

Steven Spielberg

World-renowned filmmaker Steven Spielberg has directed numerous films including *Jaws, ET the Extra Terrestrial, Jurassic Park, Saving Private Ryan* (for which he received an Academy Award for best director), and *Schindler's List* (for which he won Academy Awards for best director as well as best picture for his work as a producer). Spielberg established the Righteous Persons Foundation with all of his personal profits from *Schindler's List.* He is the founder of the Survivors of the Shoah Visual History Foundation, which has recorded over 50,000 Holocaust survivor testimonies.

This recipe is from Steven's mother, Leah Adler, who owns a restaurant in Los Angeles. Steven has built a kosher kitchen in his home just for Leah—on the chance that she will cook this or something else for him when she comes to visit.

Leah Adler's
Cheese Blintzes

Pancakes
4 eggs, beaten
1 cup milk
1 teaspoon salt
1 cup flour
Butter or shortening, for frying pancakes

Filling
1½ pounds cottage cheese
2 egg yolks, beaten
1 tablespoon butter
1 tablespoon sugar
Sour cream and strawberry preserves, for serving

1. Add milk and salt to beaten eggs. Add flour gradually and stir until smooth.
2. Combine filling ingredients and set aside.
3. Heat a heavy, 6-inch skillet, grease lightly, then pour enough batter for a thin pancake (about 2 tablespoons). Tip pan from side to side until batter covers bottom of pan. Cook on one side only, until it blisters, then remove from pan, tossing the fried side up onto a cutting board. Do not stack pancakes until cool.
4. When a number of pancakes have been fried, place a rounded tablespoon of filling in center of each pancake.
5. Fold both sides over like an envelope to enclose filling.
6. Fry in butter or shortening on both sides until golden. Serve hot with sour cream and strawberry preserves.

P.S. To be made with love.

Beverly Sills

Photo: Don Purdue

Brooklyn-born Beverly Sills, one of the great coloratura sopranos, is chairman of the board of Lincoln Center for the Performing Arts, Inc. She debuted with the San Francisco Opera in 1953 and went on to expand her repertoire to more than seventy operas. Sills has sung in virtually all of the world's leading opera houses and has recorded eighteen full-length operas and several solo recital discs. Her honors include the Presidential Medal of Freedom. Sills is the retired national chairman of the March of Dimes Foundation, for which she helped raise over eighty million dollars. The mother of four daughters and one son, she lives in New York City with her husband, Peter B. Greenough.

"Dutch Babies" Pancake

Makes a good midnight snack or Sunday brunch.

3 eggs
½ cup flour
½ cup milk
½ teaspoon salt
3 tablespoons butter, melted
Jam, stewed fruit, maple syrup, or butter, for serving

1. Preheat oven to 450°F.
2. Put an 8-inch iron skillet in freezer.
3. Combine eggs, flour, milk, and salt in blender and blend at low speed until smooth.
4. Pour melted butter into the cold iron skillet.
5. Pour batter into skillet.
6. Bake in oven until crust is brown (approximately 10 to 15 minutes). It will puff up like a soufflé.

Serve immediately with jam, stewed fruit, maple syrup, or butter.

Rick Moranis

Actor Rick Moranis has delighted audiences with his starring roles in such hit comedies as *Ghostbusters, Spaceballs, Parenthood,* and *Honey, I Shrunk the Kids.* Born in Toronto, he attended the University of Toronto, York University. He began his career in radio in 1970 as an engineer and joined SCTV (Second City Television) in 1980. There, he and fellow actor Dave Thomas created the McKenzie brothers, a comic Canadian duo. This led to *Strange Brew,* featuring the McKenzie Brothers, the first of Moranis' many films.

"When I was a young kid our whole family on my mother's side—cousins, aunts and uncles—shared a small cottage owned by my grandmother near Lake Simcoe, north of Toronto. The Passover before one particular summer, I began to drive my mother crazy by insisting on matzah brei for breakfast every day. This went on well past Passover and into the summer. Every morning the same thing would happen. The smell of matzah brei would gloriously fill the cottage, and one by one people would drift into the kitchen and make themselves their own matzah brei. The kind, old, Gentile store owner around the corner was never more confused than the summer he couldn't keep matzah in stock."

– Rick Moranis

Matzah Brei for the Other 357 Days

Matzah
Brei (If anyone knows where to get fresh brei, let me know.)
Eggs
Milk
Salt
Pepper
Butter
Scallions or chives, and parsley (optional)

1. Use 1 matzah and 1 egg per serving, 2 if you're related (in any way) to my family.
2. Soften the matzah slightly by running lukewarm water over it for a few seconds. This will open its pores (or brei) to help it absorb the egg. Use regular matzah or any kind you prefer. Break the matzah in half, wash your hands and finish the seder. No, sorry, break the matzah in inchish (inchish?) pieces and soak for a couple of minutes in a mixture of egg, a bit of milk, salt, and pepper.
3. In a nonstick pan, melt some butter (olive oil if you're Sephardic, a lot of butter if you're French). At this point you can get a bit quirky and sauté some scallions or chives, and parsley. Or if you don't want indigestion, pour the mixture into the pan and fry it. Against everything the religion has taught you, do not overcook.

Don Rickles

A talented actor and comedian known for his "insult" brand of humor, Don Rickles was born in New York City. He began his career doing stand-up comedy in small clubs and was discovered by Frank Sinatra in 1957 at Slate Brothers, a Hollywood nightclub. Sinatra promoted him to other celebrities, and two years later he appeared at the Hotel Sahara in Las Vegas. Since then, Rickles has headlined at top clubs around the country, recorded two best-selling comedy albums, and made numerous television appearances. He starred in *The Don Rickles Show* in 1968 and again in 1971-72, and the *C.P.O. Sharkey* television series in 1977-78. His movie credits include *Run Silent, Run Deep; Kelly's Heroes;* and the voice of Mr. Potatohead in both *Toy Story* and *Toy Story 2.* Rickles has been married to his wife Barbara since 1965, and they are the parents of a daughter and a son.

"Sorry no recipe or anecdote. Make one up and say it's mine."

– Don Rickles

White Lasagna for Passover
from Toby Colton

Sauce
8 tablespoons (1 stick) butter
⅓ cup plus 1 tablespoon matzah cake meal
5 cups milk (2% or whole) or 4¾ cups milk plus ¼ cup dry white Passover wine
1 to 2 teaspoons dried thyme
½ teaspoon grated nutmeg
¼ teaspoon ground black pepper
¼ teaspoon salt

Filling
1 egg (optional)
¾ pound (about 3 cups) shredded mozzarella cheese
½ cup grated Parmesan cheese
1½ pounds ricotta cheese
1 cup peeled, coarsely grated carrot
¼ teaspoon salt
6 matzahs
1 cup fresh spinach leaves, thinly sliced or minced

Topping
¼ cup grated Parmesan cheese and ¼ pound (about 1 cup) shredded mozzarella cheese, combined

1. Preheat oven to 350° F and grease a 9 x 13-inch baking pan with olive oil or butter.
2. **For sauce:** In medium saucepan, over medium heat, melt butter with cake meal. Stir and let cook 2 to 3 minutes. Add milk and spices and bring to a boil. Cook gently until sauce thickens. Remove from heat.
3. **For filling:** Combine egg, mozzarella cheese, Parmesan cheese, ricotta cheese, grated carrot, and salt. Set aside.
4. **To assemble:** Pour ½ cup of sauce in bottom of pan. Top with 2 sheets of matzah. Place half of the filling mixture on top. Sprinkle with half of the spinach. Top with 1½ cups sauce.
5. Repeat layers.
6. Top with remaining matzah, cover with remaining sauce, and sprinkle with topping.
7. Bake uncovered for 30 minutes or until it bubbles around edges. Let cool 15 to 20 minutes before cutting.

Recipe can be made ahead of time and frozen, uncooked. Defrost before baking.

Makes 8 to 10 servings.

Note: This recipe can easily be converted to a non-Passover dish. Substitute ½ cup flour for matzah cake meal. Use 9 uncooked lasagna noodles in place of matzah.

Steven Peterman

"I was born in Milwaukee, grew up on the West Side, and spent my formative years (and most Jewish holidays) making pizza at my parents' place, the legendary Pizza Wagon, where a generation of Milwaukee kids hung out, pigged out, and made out in the parking lot until my dad came out with his flashlight and sent them all home. I went to Harvard, where I continued a lifelong love of theatre culminating in a starring role as the female ingenue in the 133rd production of the Hasty Pudding Club (the country's oldest continuous college theatrical society). After six months on a kibbutz and a disastrous three-week career in law school at the University of Wisconsin (just long enough to lose my parents the entire first semester's tuition), I drove all night to New York where I spent two years at Circle in the Square

Theatre School and made my Broadway debut playing (of course) a law professor. After five years of Broadway, off Broadway, and way off Broadway, I moved to Los Angeles where in a brief while, I was playing (of course) a law school graduate in a *Hallmark Hall of Fame* production. After playing more lawyers, law students, and, when I took off my glasses, drug dealers in television shows, I started writing out of desperation with a fellow actor, Gary Dontzig (yes, another Jew). Our first television job was on an after-school show for kids called *Rocky Road.* From there we moved to a brief stay on *Full House,* a half season on *A Different World,* and then, miraculously, the first six years of *Murphy Brown,* during which we moved from the least experienced and lowest members of the writing staff to executive producers of the show. We won three Emmy Awards. We went on to rewrite the pilot and executive produce the first three years of *Suddenly Susan.* Since leaving the show, we have written a movie of the week and are working on other projects. After almost fifteen years of episodic television I'm thrilled to have a little more time with my wife, Susan, with whom I've celebrated over twenty years of marriage, and our son, Will, who's proudly showing off the broken nose he got in his first Little League practice."

"I first learned this recipe from the back of a Mueller's macaroni box when I was a starving acting student in New York. It was cheap, simple to make, and very filling during long, cold New York winters. It was also the first meal I cooked for my wife, Susan, shortly after we met in 1975. The only thing worse than dating an actor is dating an unemployed actor, so I figured a good macaroni might go further than a mediocre Macbeth. And when I set that steaming beauty down on the table (and I mean the macaroni, not Susan—this is a cookbook for God's sake), the girl was smitten.

Years later, when I became executive producer of *Murphy Brown* I cooked the dish for Candice Bergen as part of my get-to-know-me campaign, and for a brief period she thought of leaving her husband, Louis Malle, for me. I had to sit her down and tell her I loved my wife and I thought it better if we stayed just friends. Besides, this is about the only thing I can cook, and that cheese will add a lot of pounds on camera.

For three years I was executive producer of *Suddenly Susan*, and while Brooke Shields has often sidled up to me during rehearsal to whisper suggestively, "Gee, I could really go for a steaming bowl of something hot and cheesy," I have learned my lesson. This is a meal to be served only when you are serious about a commitment. With that caveat in mind, enjoy."

– Steven Peterman

Homemade Macaroni and Cheese Supreme

2 cups elbow macaroni
2 tablespoons butter
2 tablespoons flour
1 teaspoon salt
1 teaspoon mustard
2½ cups milk
2 cups (8 ounces) cheese, grated (I use sharp Wisconsin cheddar, of course!)

Topping

2 tablespoons butter
¼ cup bread crumbs

1. Preheat oven to 375°F.
2. Cook macaroni (follow directions on box).
3. In a medium saucepan, melt 2 tablespoons butter, then remove from heat.
4. Blend in flour, salt, and mustard.
5. Add milk and heat slowly, stirring frequently until slightly thickened.
6. Add cheese. *(I usually add a bit more than the 8 ounces because, like any Wisconsin native, I don't believe you can ever have too much cheese.)*
7. **For topping:** In a large pan melt butter and toast bread crumbs until light brown.
8. Put cooked macaroni into a 1½- to 2-quart casserole dish, cover with sauce, add bread crumbs to top, and bake for 20 to 25 minutes.
9. Eat immediately and burn your tongue and the roof of your mouth, or let stand for 10 minutes *(something I was usually too hungry to do)*.

Wendy Wasserstein

Photo: James Hamilton

Acclaimed playwright Wendy Wasserstein is noted for comedic plays that focus on the struggles of contemporary American women. Her plays also reflect her Jewish heritage and influences from the Russian writer Chekhov. Born in Brooklyn, Wasserstein studied at Mt. Holyoke College, City College of New York, and the Yale School of Drama. Her first major play, *Uncommon Women and Others* (1977), gained her national recognition and was televised by PBS. Other works include *Isn't It Romantic, The Sisters Rosensweig,* and *The Heidi Chronicles,* for which she won the 1989 Pulitzer Prize in drama.

"I am a very big fan of tuna fish salad on an English muffin with a cup of soup. That's about as much cooking as I do. Although I have to admit, in the spirit of Milwaukee, I'm a tremendous fan of whitefish salad, too."

– *Wendy Wasserstein*

Jerry Markbreit

Jerry Markbreit is currently a replay official for the NFL and is president of B'nai Brith's Chicago Sports Lodge. He lives with his wife, Roberta, in the Chicago area.

"I began my officiating career in 1956, working the B'nai Brith touch football league in Chicago's Grant Park. My schedule of three games each Sunday morning was the highlight of my week. I was twenty-one years old, and the players were sixteen and seventeen. I felt so important working their games that I decided to try the next level of officiating. Over the next twenty years, I worked high school, small college, and Big Ten football.

I was at the top of my game in the Big Ten, but there was one more step to climb. I applied to the National Football League and was accepted for the 1976 season. I was forty-one years old and a twenty-year veteran of football officiating. I retired from the NFL at the end of the 1998 season after twenty-three years. I was a referee for eight conference championship games and four Super Bowls."

– Jerry Markbreit

Spaghetti Casserole

This spaghetti dish gave me sustenance before games and after, when I came home drained of emotional and physical energy. I enjoy the combination of tomato soup, a favorite, with sour cream and mushrooms. It gives a certain zest to the pasta.

- 8 ounces (½ pound) spaghetti
- 1 10¾-ounce can tomato soup
- ½ pint (1 cup) sour cream
- 1 small (8-ounce) can whole mushrooms, drained
- 1 tablespoon sugar
- ½ teaspoon salt, or to taste
- 2 teaspoons grated Parmesan cheese, or to taste
- 4 slices American cheese, or to taste
- 1 tablespoon butter, plus additional for greasing pan

1. Preheat oven to 350°F. Grease casserole dish.
2. Cook spaghetti per package instructions and drain.
3. In a large mixing bowl combine soup, sour cream, mushrooms, sugar, and salt. Stir until blended.
4. Add spaghetti to soup mixture. Stir until blended.
5. Transfer spaghetti mixture to casserole dish.
6. Top with cheeses and dot with butter.
7. Bake 30 to 45 minutes, or until top is brown.

Serves 4.

Nora Ephron

Born in Manhattan and raised in Los Angeles, Nora Ephron is a three-time Academy Award nominee for best screenplay. After graduating from Wellesley College, she worked for *The New York Post.* Her screenplays include *Silkwood* (with Alice Arlen), *Heartburn,* and *When Harry Met Sally.* A successful director in a male-dominated field, she co-wrote and directed *Sleepless In Seattle* and *You've Got Mail.* Ephron is the mother of two sons and lives on Manhattan's Upper West Side.

Spaghetti with Sand

This is a simple and remarkably delicious thing to do with pasta, particularly if you're serving it with a chicken dish.

½ cup plus 2 tablespoons olive oil (not virgin!)
2 to 4 cloves garlic, peeled and slivered
1 cup good quality bread crumbs
1 pound spaghetti
Salt to taste

1. Bring a large pot (4-quart or larger) of salted water to a boil for spaghetti.
2. Heat olive oil and garlic in a skillet over medium heat. Cook gently and remove from heat when garlic browns.
3. Mix bread crumbs with 2 tablespoons of the heated oil. Spread crumbs onto a baking sheet and broil until lightly toasted, or place on toaster oven pan and toast on top brown setting. Watch carefully.
4. Cook spaghetti per package directions. Drain.
5. Toss oil, spaghetti, and bread crumbs together. Add salt to taste.

Serves 4 as a main course, 6 as a side dish.

Alfred Uhry

Writer Alfred Uhry was born in Atlanta, Georgia. His plays reflect his southern Jewish roots and are based on his family. Uhry is the author of *Driving Miss Daisy,* which won a 1988 Pulitzer Prize; his screen adaptation won an Academy Award in 1989. After the huge success of *Miss Daisy*, he was asked to write a play for the 1996 Atlanta Olympic Arts Festival. The result was the Tony Award-winning *The Last Night of Ballyhoo*. This was followed by *Parade*, another Tony winner. Uhry has written the lyrics for several Broadway musicals, including *The Robber Bridegroom*, as well as the screenplay for *Mystic Pizza*. He lives with his wife in New York.

"Brunswick Stew is old-fashioned southern cooking—a Georgia staple in pre-Civil War days. The original calls for pork shoulders and chickens and cooks all day. This version was invented by my grandmother (the inspiration for Miss Daisy), and I've modernized it to cut down on fat and cholesterol. My four daughters were crazy about it when they were kids at home. It's still great when they all come back for the weekend."

– Alfred Uhry

Brunswick Stew

1 tablespoon olive oil
1 medium onion, chopped
2 pounds ground turkey
1 15-ounce can creamed corn
1 15-ounce can crushed tomatoes
Salt and pepper to taste
A shake of hot sauce (optional)
3 cups hot, cooked rice for serving

1. In a large skillet heat olive oil. Add onions and cook over medium heat until soft.
2. In a separate skillet cook ground meat. Drain off fat and add meat to onions.
3. Add rest of ingredients and cook on medium low heat until all are blended (30 minutes).
4. Serve over rice.

Serves 4 to 6.

Barbara Walters

Barbara Walters is an ABC news correspondent and co-anchor of the ABC news magazine *20/20*. She is also well known for *The Barbara Walters Specials*. She has interviewed numerous world leaders, newsmakers, and celebrities. Among her accomplishments are the first joint interview with Egypt's President Anwar Sadat and Israel's Prime Minister Menachem Begin in November 1977, and an exclusive prime-time interview with Cuban President Fidel Castro. Born in Boston and a graduate of Sarah Lawrence College, she began her television career as a writer for *The Today Show.* In 1976, Walters was the first woman to co-host a network news program. She is the recipient of numerous awards and honorary doctoral degrees, including one from Ben-Gurion University in Jerusalem. She has one daughter.

Mother's Stuffed Cabbage Rolls

2 heads (2 pounds each) green cabbage
6 quarts boiling water
3 pounds lean ground chuck
Salt to taste
¾ teaspoon pepper
2 teaspoons celery salt, or to taste
½ cup ketchup
2 eggs
½ cup crushed, unsalted crackers

Sauce
3 cups chopped onion
2 12-ounce bottles (2 cups each) chili sauce
1 12-ounce jar (1 cup) grape jelly
¼ cup water

1. Preheat oven to 375°F. Lightly grease one 11½ x 12 x 2¼-inch roasting pan or two 13 x 9 x 2-inch baking pans.
2. Cut out and discard hard center core of cabbage. Place cabbage in large kettle. Pour 6 quarts boiling water over it. Let stand until leaves are flexible and can easily be removed from head, about 5 minutes. Remove from hot water and separate and drain leaves. If necessary, return cabbage to hot water to soften inner leaves. Repeat with second cabbage.
3. In large bowl combine meat, salt, pepper, celery salt, ketchup, eggs, and crackers. Mix with hands just until mixture is well combined.
4. Using a ¼-cup measure, scoop up a scant ¼ cup of the meat mixture. With hands, form into rolls 3 inches long and 1 inch wide, making about 28 rolls in all. Place each meat roll on a drained cabbage leaf. Fold top of leaf over meat, then fold in sides and roll into an oblong. Continue rolling remaining meat rolls and cabbage leaves.
5. Spread chopped onion evenly in bottom of pan(s). Arrange cabbage rolls in neat rows on top of onion.
6. **For sauce:** In a 2-quart saucepan, combine chili sauce, grape jelly, and ¼ cup water. Heat over medium heat, stirring, until jelly melts. Pour over cabbage rolls. Cover pan tightly with foil.
7. Bake for 2 hours. Remove foil. Brush rolls with sauce. Continue to bake, uncovered, 20 to 40 minutes or until sauce is thick and syrupy and cabbage rolls are glazed. Spoon sauce over rolls and serve.

Makes 28 cabbage rolls to serve 14.

Jane E. Brody

Born in New York City, Jane Brody received her M.S. from the University of Wisconsin School of Journalism. A science and medical writer for *The New York Times* since 1965, she has also written several books about health and cooking including *Jane Brody's Good Food Book*. Brody has received numerous writing awards. She currently resides in Brooklyn, New York, with her family.

"This recipe is my favorite—from my Jewish childhood, just like my Grandma used to make. It is a beloved remnant from my family's Eastern European origins."

– Jane E. Brody

Stuffed cabbage contains lots of cancer-preventing cabbage and a moderate amount of beef. It can be prepared weeks ahead and frozen (reheating actually improves the flavor). I have often made double, triple, even quadruple the quantity to serve at parties. It goes well with mashed potatoes, noodles, or rice. Preparation tip: The size of the cabbage rolls can be varied; if you prefer small ones, buy two or more small heads of cabbage and use the smaller leaves for rolling. If made ahead of time, prepare the complete recipe before refrigerating or freezing it, and simply reheat the stuffed cabbage in a covered pot in the oven before serving it.

Sweet-and-Sour Stuffed Cabbage

1 large head cabbage (2 or 3 pounds)
2 tablespoons margarine
2 large onions, sliced
1 16-ounce can tomatoes with their juice, coarsely chopped
Salt to taste (optional)
½ teaspoon freshly ground black pepper, divided
Beef bones, about 1 pound (optional)
1 pound very lean ground beef
¼ cup grated onion
3 tablespoons uncooked rice (white or brown)
3 tablespoons water
1 egg
2 cups (approximately) boiling broth
⅓ cup raisins
¼ cup fresh lemon juice
¼ to ½ cup honey to taste

1. Boil the whole cabbage in a large pot of water for 5 to 10 minutes to soften the leaves. When cabbage is cool enough to handle, gently remove leaves, taking care not to tear them. As you get down into the cabbage, you may have to reboil it for a few minutes to soften inner leaves. Use only the more tender, whitish leaves for rolling, and shred tough outer leaves and the very small inner ones for the sauce.
2. Melt margarine in a deep, heavy saucepan, Dutch oven, or roasting pan. Add onions and brown lightly. Add tomatoes with their juice, about ½ teaspoon of salt (if desired), ¼ teaspoon of the pepper, beef bones (if desired), and shredded cabbage. Bring mixture to a boil, reduce heat to low, and cook mixture, uncovered, for about 30 minutes.
3. Meanwhile, prepare cabbage rolls. In a medium bowl, combine beef, grated onion, rice, water, egg, another ½ teaspoon of salt, and remaining ¼ teaspoon of pepper. Depending on the size roll desired, place from 1½ to 3 tablespoons of meat mixture toward the stem end of each cabbage leaf. Fold in shorter sides of the leaf, then roll from stem end to outer edge, enclosing meat and short ends of the leaf to form a fairly tight, compact roll or ball.
4. Add broth to sauce, mixing well. Then add cabbage rolls to sauce, arranging them so they are surrounded by the sauce. Cover pan and cook stuffed cabbage slowly over low heat for 1½ hours.
5. Add raisins, lemon juice, and honey (start with ¼ cup and taste sauce before adding more), distributing these ingredients as evenly as possible. Cook cabbage, uncovered, 30 minutes longer.

Makes 12 to 18 medium-sized rolls.

David H. Levy

Photo: Wendee Wallach-Levy

One of the world's foremost astronomers, David H. Levy is credited with and tied for the third largest number of comet discoveries since records have been kept. Levy has discovered twenty-one comets, thirteen with Eugene and Carolyn Shoemaker, and eight using his own backyard telescope. With the Shoemakers at the Palomar Observatory in California, he discovered Shoemaker-Levy 9, the comet that collided with Jupiter in 1994. Asteroid 3673 Levy was named in his honor. Born in Montreal, Canada, Levy has never taken an astronomy course. He holds both a B.A. and an M.A. in English. Levy is the science editor of *PARADE* magazine, a columnist for *Sky and Telescope,* and the author of twenty books including *Comets: Creators and Destroyers.* He received an Emmy in 1997 for his work on the television documentary *Three Minutes to Impact.* He currently resides in Vail, Arizona, with his wife, Wendee, and their two dogs.

Mexican Meat Mixture

1 pound lean ground beef
1 pound ground turkey
1 to 2 packages taco seasoning mix (dry), about 1 ounce each
1 4-ounce can diced green chilies, undrained
2 16-ounce cans black beans, undrained
1 16-ounce can refried beans, black or pinto (optional)
Corn chips or flour tortillas (optional)

1. Brown beef and turkey. Discard drippings.
2. Add taco seasoning mix. Follow directions on package.
3. Add green chilies and black beans. Let simmer until heated through.

Optional: For a thicker mixture, add refried beans and heat until warmed.

Serve:

A) As a dip with chips;

B) As a nacho topping over chips;

C) Right out of the bowl; or

D) If thick enough, wrapped into a burrito.

Makes about 1½ quarts.

Leon Uris

Photo: Jerry Bauer

Over 150 million copies of Leon Uris' books have been sold in more than twenty-five languages. The author of many acclaimed historical novels, he was born in Baltimore. His first book, *Battle Cry*, based on his service in the Marine Corps from 1942 to 1945, was published in 1953 and was an immediate success. In 1956, he covered an Arab-Israeli conflict as a war correspondent, which resulted in the publication of *Exodus* in 1958. A novelization of the founding of Israel, *Exodus* became one of the best-selling books of all time. Uris' other works include the novels *Mila 18* and *A God in Ruins*, as well as screenplays for *Exodus* and *Gunfight at the OK Corral.* He received the Jabotinsky Medal of the State of Israel in 1980. Uris and his wife Jill, a photographer, have collaborated on several books. Married for over thirty years and the parents of three children, they live in Colorado.

Osso Buco

1 tablespoon oil
½ cup chopped onion
½ cup chopped celery
1 tablespoon minced, fresh basil
1 clove garlic, crushed
1 pinch dried thyme
1 dried bay leaf
1 cup white wine
Pepper to taste
2 veal shanks, 1½ inches thick (¾ pound each)
2 or 3 tomatoes, chopped
1 carrot, peeled and cut into small pieces
Salt to taste
2 cups hot cooked rice, couscous, quinoa, or mashed potatoes, for serving

1. In a large pot, heat oil. Add onion, celery, basil, garlic, thyme, bay leaf, and pepper. Cook, stirring, until vegetables are softened.
2. Add wine and veal shanks and cook, covered, for 20 minutes.
3. Turn veal over. Add tomatoes and carrots. Cook, covered, over medium to low heat for an additional 20 to 40 minutes until veal is tender, stirring occasionally to prevent sticking. Add salt to taste.
4. Serve in large soup bowls over rice, couscous, quinoa, or mashed potatoes.

Jim Abrahams

Photo: Melinda Sue Gordon

Screenwriter, director, and producer Jim Abrahams' long list of credits includes *Hot Shots, Part I* and *Hot Shots, Part Deux* (1991 and 1993), and *Welcome Home Roxy Carmichael.* Milwaukee-born Abrahams co-founded the storefront comedy troupe The Kentucky Fried Theater. When filmed as the *Kentucky Fried Movie,* it became one of the most successful independent films of all time. The troupe went on to write and direct other successful comedy spoofs including *Airplane* and the *Naked Gun* series. Abrahams also established The Charlie Foundation To Help Cure Pediatric Epilepsy.

"At the age of seven, I learned this from my mom, whose motto used to be:

'If you want it clean, go wash it;
If you want it pressed, go iron it;
If you want it cooked, go cook it.' "

– Jim Abrahams

Pot Roast

1 3-pound chuck roast
1 onion, diced
6 carrots, diced
1 12-ounce bottle French dressing

1. Preheat oven to 275°.
2. Brown roast in oven-safe pan (use a little oil if necessary).
3. Add onion and carrots. Cover with entire bottle of dressing.
4. Bake, covered, for 5 hours.

Serves 4 to 6.

David Zucker

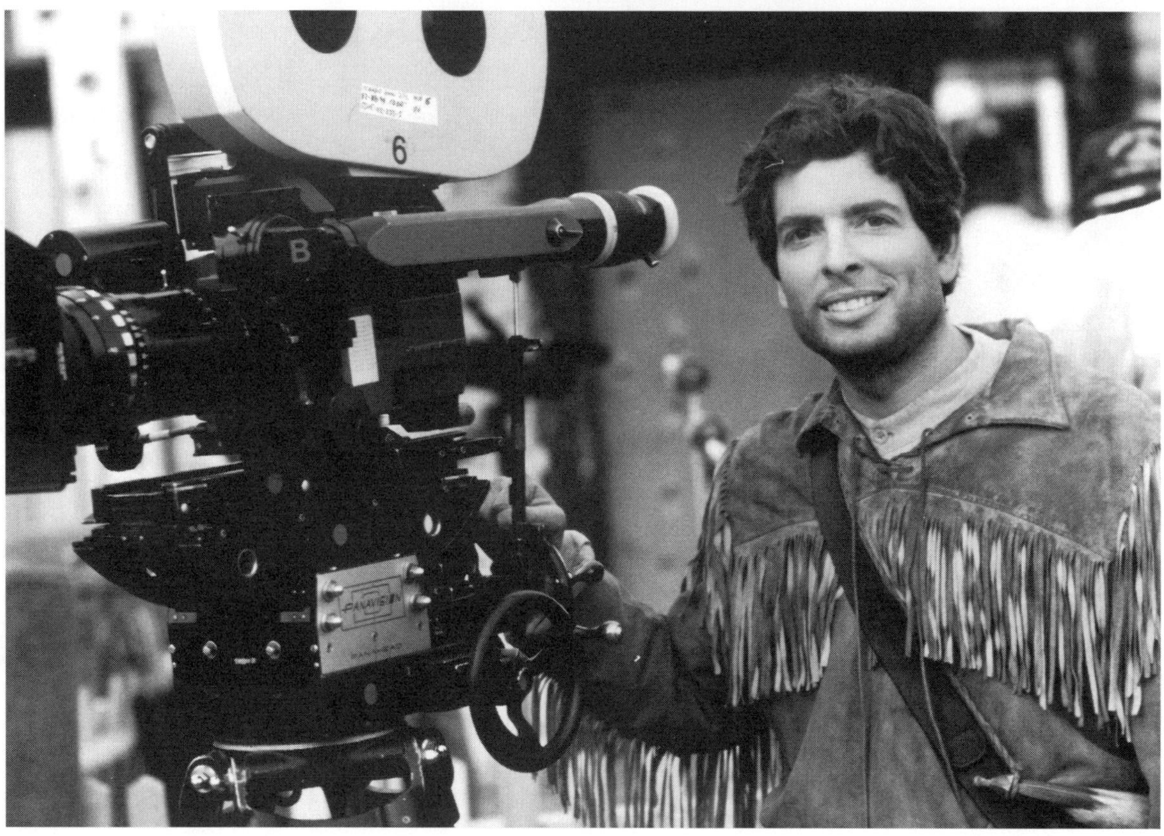

Milwaukee native David Zucker has co-written, co-directed, directed, produced, executive produced, and performed in nine films that are considered some of the most successful and memorable spoof-comedies of recent years. Originally part of the theatrical troupe Kentucky Fried Theater, Zucker's films include *Airplane!, Top Secret, Naked Gun, Naked Gun 2-1/2, Naked Gun 33-1/3*, and *Ruthless People*.

"When I was a kid growing up in Shorewood, Wisconsin, at least once a week Mom would serve us a dinner of tongue. Being only kids, and having no idea how disgusting that was, we loved it—mainly because it tasted so great. Unfortunately, over the years, the popularity of tongue seems to have waned, due perhaps to vegetarianism, the animal rights movement, or maybe just the realization of what the hell we were eating. In any case, I couldn't imagine any recipe that would make a more satisfying repast than my mom's tongue."

– David Zucker

Fresh Tongue and Sauce

Tongue
1 beef tongue
1 large onion, peeled and quartered
2 large bay leaves
4 whole cloves
½ cup celery tops
1 heaping tablespoon salt

Sauce
4 tablespoons margarine, divided
½ pound fresh mushrooms, sliced, or one 8-ounce can sliced mushrooms
3 tablespoons flour
1 10½-ounce can beef bouillon
2 to 4 tablespoons slivered almonds, for garnish

1. **For tongue:** In a large soup pot, cover tongue with cold water. Bring to a boil. Add onion, bay leaves, cloves, celery tops, and salt.
2. Cover and simmer about 50 minutes per pound until done (test with fork tip at the end of the tongue).
3. Cool and peel while still warm. Cut away bones and fat from base. Slice on diagonal.
4. **For sauce:** In a large skillet over medium heat, melt 1 tablespoon margarine. Add raw mushrooms and sauté until tender. Transfer to a bowl and set aside. If using canned mushrooms, skip this step.
5. In the same pan, over medium heat, melt remaining 3 tablespoons margarine and heat until golden. Stir in and brown flour.
6. Slowly add and stir in beef bouillon.
7. Add sautéed mushrooms and any accumulated juices, or canned mushrooms with liquid.
8. Heat the sliced tongue and sauce together.
9. Add slivered almonds when ready to serve.

Henry Winkler

Henry Winkler, an award-winning actor, producer, and director, works in film, television, and on stage. On his twenty-eighth birthday, Winkler was cast in the role of Arthur "Fonzie" Fonzarelli and rocketed into stardom with his portrayal of the super-cool biker on the television sitcom *Happy Days*. The show ran from 1974 to 1984, and "The Fonz" became such an icon of pop culture that his leather jacket resides in the Smithsonian's National Museum of American History. Winkler is also widely recognized for his contributions to quality educational programming for children and his active involvement with many children's organizations and charities. He received a Master of Fine Arts from Yale School of Drama. Winkler and his wife have three children. When asked how he would like to be remembered, he has said "as a good dad."

"It is my pleasure to send along this recipe. My family uses this salad all summer long with delicious success. I hope it makes your tongue happy."

– Henry Winkler

Mexican Salad

Dressing
1½ cups mayonnaise
7 ounces (about ¾ cup) green chili salsa
⅓ cup ketchup
½ teaspoon chili powder

Mix all ingredients together and chill.

Salad
1 to 2 heads romaine lettuce, broken into ½-inch pieces
2 cans sliced black olives, drained
1 large red onion, diced
½ pound grated sharp Cheddar cheese
1 4-ounce can diced green chiles
1 to 2 bags Doritos chips, crumbled
2 avocados, peeled and diced

Toss all but chips and avocados together. Pour dressing over salad and top with chips and avocados. Serve immediately.

"Eat in health!"

Ellen Taus

Photo: Fred R. Conrad

Ellen Taus is chief financial officer of the Internet business unit of *The New York Times,* Times Company Digital. This unit operates nearly 50 Web sites, including those of *The Times* and *The Boston Globe*. Prior to holding this position, she was treasurer and vice president of The New York Times Co. Taus was also vice president of corporate finance at R.H. Macy, and chief financial officer at the American Museum of the Moving Image. She graduated from Northwestern University, received an M.B.A. from Columbia, and completed the executive program at Stanford. Taus lives in New York with her husband.

"This is one of the first recipes I used from *The New York Times* after moving to New York in 1980. The torn-out newsprint with the recipe is now yellow with age. I've served the salad many times, usually to raves, at book clubs or other informal gatherings. Little did I know when I saved this scrap of paper that I would eventually be working at *The Times*!"

– Ellen Taus

Warm Spring Salad

Salad
¾ cup raw, long grain rice
1½ cups water
1 tablespoon olive oil
10 ounces skinless, boneless chicken breast
6 ounces portobello mushrooms, cleaned, trimmed, and sliced
1 pound asparagus, cleaned, trimmed, and cut on the diagonal into 1-inch pieces

Dressing
1 tablespoon olive oil
¼ cup balsamic vinegar
Salt and pepper to taste
12 Greek or Italian olives, pitted
¼ cup finely chopped red onion
1 clove garlic, minced
2 tablespoons fresh snipped oregano or ½ teaspoon dried oregano

1. **For salad:** Combine rice and water in pot. Bring to boil, then cover and simmer for 17 minutes. Remove from heat (leave cover on pot).
2. In nonstick skillet, sauté chicken breasts in 1 tablespoon olive oil, browning on both sides for 7 to 10 minutes. Remove from pan and set aside.
3. In same skillet, sauté mushrooms until soft, about 5 minutes.
4. Steam or blanch asparagus until bright green and tender-crisp. Drain well.
5. **For dressing:** In large serving bowl, whisk together oil, vinegar, salt, and pepper. Stir in olives, onion, garlic, and oregano.
6. Cut chicken into julienne strips.
7. Add chicken, rice, mushrooms, and asparagus to serving bowl and toss gently. Serve at room temperature with crusty bread.

Serves 4.

Jerry Reinsdorf

Brooklyn-born attorney, accountant, and real estate executive Jerry Reinsdorf has been chairman of the Chicago Bulls since 1985 and chairman of the Chicago White Sox since 1981. He attended George Washington University and received his law degree from Northwestern University. He is currently serving a third four-year term on major league baseball's prestigious Executive Council. During his tenure as chairman, the Bulls won six World Championships for Chicago. Reinsdorf is active in philanthropic and city-building affairs and has sponsored an innovative reading program in the public schools. He is the recipient of many interfaith and charitable honors, including awards from the Cystic Fibrosis Foundation, the National Jewish Sporting Hall of Fame, and the Trial Lawyers Club of Chicago.

The Perfect Hot Dog

Ingredients
One (or two if available) baseball game(s)
Tickets to the game(s) for everyone whose company you enjoy
Enough money for Best Kosher hot dogs for everyone
Sunshine and warmth (to taste)
A win for the home team (the preferred garnish if available)

Preparation
Put tickets in friends' hands.
Give money for hot dogs to vendor.
Allow friends and hot dogs to blend for length of game(s).

Beverly Sills
Judy Blume
Dean Ornish
Andrew Weil
Edward Koch
Herb Kohl
Don Rickles
Michael Feldman
Ben Sidran
Paul Newman
Rick Moranis
Joel Siegel
Barbara Barrie
Rabbi Marc Gellman
Art Spiegelman
Joan Zakon Borysenko
Abigail Van Buren
John E. Spero
Jeffrey Blumkin
Jerry Stiller
Donalee Patinkin Rubin
Mandy Patinkin
Arlen Specter
Robert Klein
Edward Asner
Mollie Katzen
Steven Spielberg
Billy Joel
Al Clark
Steven Peterman
Jessie Davis
Nora Ephron
Faye Kellerman
Barbara Walters
Susan Isaacs
Wendy Selig-Prieb
Russel Feingold
Tana Hoban
Ben & Jerry
David Zucker
Henry Winkler
Claudia Cohen
Florence Eiseman
Jeffrey Cohen
Dana Goldstein
Alfred Uhry
Marjorie Bialik
David A. Adler
Ruth Pransky
Anita Diamant
Susan Stamberg
Ellen Bravo
Theodore Bikel
Bernie Siegel
Charlotte Rae
Itzhak Perlman
Robert Pinsky
Susan Estrich
Shecky Greene
Aaron Sorkin
Herb Kohl
David H. Levy
Joan Nathan
Roberta Peters
Elaine Konigsburg
Charlotte Zucker
Ellen Frass
Jim Abrahams
Joseph Lieberman
Janie E. Bondy

Side Dishes

Edward Asner

Photo: Dana Gluckstein

Actor Edward Asner has appeared in numerous motion pictures and television shows, including two miniseries, *Rich Man, Poor Man* and *Roots*. But he is undoubtedly best-known for his roles as the loveable, grumpy Mr. Grant on *The Mary Tyler Moore Show* (1970-1977) and the crusading newspaperman in the spin-off series *Lou Grant* (1977-1982). The recipient of five Golden Globe Awards and seven Emmy Awards, Asner was national president of the Screen Actors Guild from 1981 to 1985, and was inducted into the Television Academy Hall of Fame in 1996.

Balsamic Roasted New Potatoes

Edward Asner's Favorite Potato Recipe

It's a wonderful, low-fat dish that goes with anything.

2 tablespoons olive oil
2 pounds small new potatoes, washed, patted dry, and quartered, or, if using larger potatoes, cut into 1-inch pieces
1 tablespoon minced garlic
1 tablespoon minced shallots
1 teaspoon fresh thyme
1 teaspoon minced rosemary
⅛ teaspoon fresh-ground nutmeg
¼ cup balsamic vinegar
Salt and pepper

1. Preheat oven to 400° F. Place baking rack in lower third of oven.
2. Heat olive oil in a 12-inch skillet over medium-high heat. Add potatoes, garlic, and shallots. Toss in skillet until well mixed. Add thyme, rosemary, and nutmeg. Toss well. When potatoes are hot, transfer to baking pan and spread in single layer. (This part of the recipe can be made several hours ahead of time.)
3. Place pan on rack in lower third of oven. Roast potatoes until golden and just tender, about 25 minutes, turning once midway.
4. Add vinegar. Toss well. Season to taste with salt and pepper. Return to oven until sizzling, about 7 minutes. Serve immediately.

Serves 6.

Anita Diamant

The Red Tent, a story based on the biblical story of Dinah, is Anita Diamant's first novel. She is also the author of six books about contemporary Jewish life, including *Living a Jewish Life* and *The New Jewish Parenting Book*. Her work has appeared in such publications as *The Boston Globe Magazine* and *Parenting*. Diamant lives in Newton, Massachusetts, with her husband and daughter.

"I write about food a lot. This is no surprise. After all, I'm Jewish. The people of the book are also the people of the knife and fork.

This passion for eating is probably rooted in the Jewish dietary laws. Our tradition demands that we pay extraordinary attention to what goes into our mouths: 'yes' to tuna but 'no' to catfish, 'yes' to chicken but 'no' to dove. The point of all the rules and regulations has never been health; there is nothing life-threatening about spaghetti carbonara.

Kashrut is simply a perpetual poke in the ribs from On High. As you consider ordering the sweet-and-sour spareribs, a still, small voice pipes up: 'Hey, Jewish person. What are you doing?'

Historically, the dietary laws were a form of social control that kept us from chowing down with the neighbors, and made us dependent upon one another for meat as well as hospitality. It was also one of the rabbi's main jobs; somebody had to rule on the permissibility of this particular chicken or that newfangled cheese.

But however we understand, obey, and/or ignore the laws of kashrut, Jews still tend to think, argue, and kvell about food as though culinary decisions were matters of surpassing importance. Thus it is that cookbooks are not trivial but scriptural!

I hope this cookbook has a whole chapter dedicated to the potato. Jews are good at potatoes, as in latkes, knishes, kugels, soups, salads. Potatoes also make Passover bearable. Here is a recipe for all year round. And it's even *pareve*. What a *mechiaeh!*"

– ***Anita Diamant***

Trio of Roasted Potatoes

6 tablespoons olive oil
3½ pounds russet potatoes, peeled and cubed
2 pounds yams, peeled and cubed
2 pounds sweet potatoes, peeled and cubed
¼ cup fat drippings from turkey, or olive oil
¼ cup mixed herbs (thyme, marjoram, sage), finely chopped
3 tablespoons garlic, minced
Salt and pepper

1. Preheat oven to 400°F. Position racks in bottom third and top third of oven. Brush each of 2 heavy, large-rimmed baking sheets with 1 tablespoon olive oil.
2. Place remaining 4 tablespoons of olive oil in a very large bowl. Add all remaining ingredients and toss to coat well. Divide potato mixture between prepared baking sheets.
3. Roast potatoes 45 minutes, stirring occasionally. Reverse position of sheets and continue to roast until potatoes are golden brown and tender, stirring occasionally, about 30 minutes longer. Transfer potatoes to bowl and serve.

Serves 10.

Steven Raichlen

Photo: Andrew Melick

Steven Raichlen is a cookbook author and syndicated columnist. His books include *High-Flavor, Low-Fat Cooking,* which won a James Beard Award. He lives with his wife in Coconut Grove, Florida.

"Here's what happens when a nice Jewish boy from Baltimore moves to Miami, America's tropical hotspot. Things are different here in South Florida. The food is certainly different. Just visit a local supermarket: You'll find all sorts of exotic produce, like yucca (cassava root) and goniatos (South American sweet potatoes).

When I was writing my book *Miami Spice* (1994 winner of an IACP/Julia Child Award), I put a tropical twist on everything I cooked. Even the favorite Jewish Hanukkah dish, latkes. I took to making latkes with sweet potatoes, which gives them a whole new dimension and flavor. You'll love the earthy sweetness of these potato pancakes, not to mention their crisp texture. Try them. I promise you, Hanukkah will never be the same!"

– Steven Raichlen

Sweet Potato Latkes

Latkes, potato pancakes, are a specialty of the Jewish restaurants on Miami Beach, where they're eaten not only at Hanukkah, but all year long. Sweet potatoes give the recipe a Southern twist.

1 large sweet potato (about 1 pound), peeled
1 very small onion
1 egg, beaten
½ teaspoon baking powder
2 to 3 tablespoons flour or matzah meal
About 2 cups vegetable oil, for frying
Confectioners' sugar, applesauce, and/or sour cream, for serving

1. Shred the sweet potato and onion on the julienne disk of a food processor or on the coarse side of a hand grater.
2. Toss together the potato, onion, egg, and baking powder in a mixing bowl. Stir in enough of the flour to hold the mixture together.
3. Just before serving, pour the oil to a depth of at least 1 inch in a frying pan or electric skillet and heat to 350°F. Using 2 spoons, form the sweet potato mixture into 3-inch pancakes. Lower these into the fat. Fry the latkes, 4 at a time, turning with a slotted spoon or wire skimmer, until golden brown on both sides, about 2 minutes total.
4. Using a skimmer or slotted spoon, transfer the latkes to paper towels to drain. Sprinkle with confectioners' sugar and serve with applesauce and/or sour cream.

Makes 8 to 10 latkes.

Mayim Bialik

California-born Mayim Bialik started acting when she was eleven years old and is perhaps best-known for her starring role in the hit teen sitcom *Blossom*. She is also well known for her portrayal of the Bette Midler character *"C.C."* as a child in the film *Beaches*. Bialik has had roles and guest appearances on television's *MacGyver, Murphy Brown, Empty Nest, Webster,* and the horror movie *Pumpkinhead*.

"Attached is my recipe for Matzah Ball Tzimmes with Apricot Sauce. Here's the story about this dish. One of my oldest friend's mom is a chef. She gave me the recipe and my Ema (mother) and I make it for Pesach. It sounds a bit complicated, but it's so much fun to make and incredible tasting—it's well worth the effort. We get requests to make this tzimmes year round; so far, we make everyone wait for Pesach."

– *Mayim Bialik*

Sweet Potato Matzah Ball Tzimmes with Apricot Sauce

Matzah Balls
2 large, red-skinned sweet potatoes (a.k.a. yams), about 1½ pounds
1¼ cups unsalted matzah meal
5 large eggs
8 tablespoons unsalted pareve margarine, divided
2½ tablespoons sugar
1¾ teaspoons coarse salt
1¼ teaspoons ground ginger

Apricot Sauce
3 cups apple juice
1 6-ounce package dried apricots, chopped
1 cinnamon stick, broken in half
4 tablespoons unsalted pareve margarine
⅓ cup apricot jam
Chopped mint for garnish (optional)

1. **For matzah balls:** Pierce potatoes with a fork. Microwave on high until tender (about 10 minutes), turning once, or roast in 350°F oven until tender (about 45 minutes). Cut them in half and scoop out enough potato to make 1¼ cups. Let cool.
2. Mix potato, matzah meal, eggs, 2½ tablespoons margarine, sugar, salt, and ginger in food processor, mixer, or with a fork until well blended. Transfer this mixture to a bowl. Cover and chill until firm, about 1 hour (or even overnight if you want!).
3. Using wet hands, roll generous teaspoonfuls of matzah mixture into little balls. Place balls on a large platter or baking pan until all balls are rolled.
4. Cook one-third of the matzah balls in a large pot of slightly salted boiling water, covered, until tender, about 6 minutes. Using a slotted spoon, transfer to a second platter or large baking pan. Repeat with the remaining balls. Let stand until firm, at least 30 minutes.
5. **For sauce:** Bring apple juice and apricots to a boil in a small saucepan. Remove from heat. Cover and steep until apricots are tender, about 10 minutes. Drain juices into a medium saucepan and add the cinnamon. Add 4 tablespoons margarine and the jam. Simmer over medium heat until reduced to ¾ cup, about 20 minutes. Return the apricots to the sauce.
6. Melt 5½ tablespoons of margarine in a large skillet over medium-high heat. Add one-third of the matzah balls. Sauté until they start to brown, about 4 minutes. Transfer to a 13 x 9 x 2-inch glass baking dish. Repeat with the rest of the matzah balls.
7. Preheat oven to 350°F. Spoon sauce over matzah balls. Bake until heated through, about 20 minutes. Top with mint.

Enjoy!

Robert Klein

Acclaimed for his intelligent style of humor, comedian and actor Robert Klein was born in the Bronx. A graduate of Alfred University and Yale Drama School, he began his career with Chicago's Second City comedy troupe. Klein received a Tony nomination for best actor in a Broadway musical for *They're Playing Our Song,* as well as an Outer Critics Circle Award for his role in *The Sisters Rosensweig.* His film credits include *The Owl and the Pussycat.* He has entertained audiences many times on *The Ed Sullivan Show,* the *Tonight Show,* and *Late Night with David Letterman,* and has starred in numerous HBO comedy specials.

"Mother cooked this as a staple three times a week. She was born in New York, but all four of my grandparents were born in Hungary."

– *Robert Klein*

Hungarian Potatoes

Potatoes*
Oil
Onions, finely chopped
Red pepper
Garlic
Paprika
Salt to taste (optional)

1. In a medium saucepan, boil potatoes in salted water until tender. Drain, saving a little cooking water.
2. While potatoes are cooking, heat oil in a large skillet. Sauté onions, pepper, and garlic with a liberal dose of paprika (for color) until tender and brown. Remove from heat.
3. Mash potatoes into sautéed vegetables, adding a little cooking liquid if too dry. Add salt to taste.

**Editor's note: Our testers used the following quantities:*

2 pounds potatoes, peeled and cut into 1-inch cubes
¼ cup oil
2½ cups finely chopped onions
1 large, sweet red bell pepper, chopped (1¼ to 1½ cups)
1½ tablespoons minced garlic
4 teaspoons sweet, Hungarian paprika, or to taste
1 teaspoon salt

Makes 4 to 6 servings.

Darra Goldstein

Darra Goldstein is a professor of Russian at Williams College in Massachusetts who has written about Russian literature, culture, art, and cuisine. Her cookbooks include *A Taste of Russia* and *The Georgian Feast*, winner of the Julia Child Award for 1993 Best Cookbook of the Year. She received an A.B. from Vassar College in 1973 and a Ph.D. from Stanford in 1983.

"Jews have been living in the Republic of Georgia for over two thousand years. In fact, in 1998, Georgia celebrated the twenty-six hundredth anniversary of Jewish settlement in Georgia. Many Jews lived in the mountain village of Oni, and they were said to be descendants of one of the lost tribes of Israel. This delicious recipe is typical of Georgian food, which uses lots of walnuts and fresh herbs."

– ***Darra Goldstein***

Potato Pancake (*Labda*)

Labda is a Passover specialty of the Georgian Jews, but this large, rich pancake makes a quick and filling supper any time of year.

1 pound potatoes
1 cup finely chopped walnuts
2 tablespoons finely chopped parsley
½ teaspoon salt
Freshly ground pepper
3 large eggs, beaten
2 tablespoons butter
2 tablespoons corn oil

1. Boil potatoes until tender.
2. Peel and mash potatoes.
3. Stir in walnuts, parsley, salt, pepper to taste, and eggs, mixing well.
4. In a 10-inch nonstick skillet with sloping sides, melt 1 tablespoon of butter with 1 tablespoon of oil. When hot, spoon pancake batter into pan, pressing down with a spatula to form an even cake. Cook over medium-high heat for about 4 minutes, or until bottom of pancake is brown and crusty.
5. Slide pancake onto a platter.
6. Melt remaining butter in the skillet and add remaining oil. Invert pancake into skillet and fry the other side until brown, about 4 minutes more.
7. Slide out onto a platter, cut into wedges and serve.

Serves 8.

Editor's note: If using any pan other than nonstick, heat pan until hot enough for a few drops of water to dance in the pan. Add fat and proceed with the recipe.

Joey Bishop

Comedian Joey Bishop was born in the Bronx and grew up in Philadelphia. He is probably best known for being a member of the "Rat Pack," a group of entertainers comprised of Bishop, Frank Sinatra, Dean Martin, Sammy Davis, Jr., and Peter Lawford, that was hugely popular in the late '50s and early '60s. Bishop guest-hosted the *Jack Paar Show* as well as *The Tonight Show*, ultimately hosting his own late-night program, *The Joey Bishop Show*. He has appeared in numerous films, including *A Guide for the Married Man* and *The Naked and The Dead* (of which he has said that he played both roles). He lives in Newport Beach, California, with Sylvia, his wife of over fifty years.

"I was the youngest of five children and still feel I never got my fair amount of kugel."

– Joey Bishop

Potato Kugel (Pudding)

1½ pounds potatoes, peeled
1 small onion, peeled
1 tablespoon chicken fat (rendered)
1 egg, beaten
Salt and pepper to taste

1. Cook potatoes in salted, boiling water until tender.
2. Drain potatoes and mash until smooth.
3. Grate onion and add to potatoes. Add chicken fat, egg, salt, and pepper. Mix very well.
4. Put mixture into a greased 1½-quart casserole or 9-inch square baking dish.
5. Bake in a cool (300°F) oven for 2 hours.

Mollie Katzen

Cookbook author and illustrator Mollie Katzen was born in Rochester, New York, and received a bachelor's degree from the San Francisco Art Institute. She began cooking as a child, helping her mother braid challah. In 1973, Katzen and six others opened the famed Moosewood Restaurant in Ithaca, New York. This resulted in the publication of the Ten Speed Press edition of *Moosewood Cookbook* in 1977. Other cookbooks followed, including *The Enchanted Broccoli Forest* and *Mollie Katzen's Vegetable Heaven*, all illustrated with her drawings, watercolors, and pastels. Katzen has also hosted her own cooking show on public television. She currently resides with her husband and two children near Berkeley, California.

Tante Malka's Potato Kugel Deluxe

A little oil for the pan
4 medium-sized potatoes
3 tablespoons butter or canola oil
3 cups minced onion
½ pound mushrooms, minced
2 teaspoons salt
3 large cloves garlic, minced
Fresh black pepper to taste
2 tablespoons minced fresh dill
4 eggs, beaten (okay to delete yolks)
1 cup sour cream (optional)
½ cup bread crumbs or matzah meal
Paprika (optional) and a little extra oil (optional), for the top

1. Preheat oven to 375°F. Lightly oil a 9 x 13-inch baking pan.
2. Scrub and coarsely grate the potatoes. (A food processor with the grating attachment works beautifully.) Set aside.
3. Melt butter or heat oil in a large, deep skillet. Add onion and sauté over medium heat for about 5 minutes. Add potatoes, mushrooms, and salt, and sauté about 10 minutes more. Stir in the garlic during the last minute or so. Remove from heat and transfer to a large bowl.
4. Add remaining ingredients and mix well. Spread evenly into prepared pan, and dust top with paprika. Bake for 1 to 1¼ hours until crisp on top. For an extra crisp top, brush with a little extra oil halfway through the baking. Cut into squares, and serve hot or warm.

Makes about 6 servings.

Jesse Levis

Cleveland Indians catcher Jesse Levis, who was born and raised in Philadelphia, has had a lifelong love of baseball. He played Little League and American Legion ball as a boy, three years of high school ball, and college ball at the University of North Carolina, where he majored in communications. Levis was drafted by the Cleveland Indians in 1989 and made his major league debut on April 24, 1992. In 1996, he was traded to the Milwaukee Brewers, where he played for three years. Levis set a club record with forty-five pinch-hit at bats in 1997. He recorded eleven pinch hits in 1997, as he had in 1996, which ranks second in Brewers history. Levis lives in the Philadelphia area with his wife, Joan, a physical therapist.

Potato Zucchini Kugel

6 medium potatoes, peeled
1 medium onion, peeled
3 medium zucchini, peeled
6 eggs, beaten
2 tablespoons oil
1 teaspoon salt
⅛ teaspoon pepper
½ cup flour (optional)

1. Preheat oven to 350°F. Thoroughly grease a 13 x 9 x 2-inch pan.
2. Place peeled potatoes in cold water.
3. Grate onion, zucchini, and potatoes (a food processor works well).
4. Transfer vegetables to a large bowl.
5. In a separate bowl, mix eggs, oil, salt, pepper, and flour.
6. Combine all ingredients.
7. Bake 1 to 1¼ hours, until golden brown.

Note: For a crustier dish, bake in a preheated deep casserole pan, metal or cast-iron. Oil pan immediately before adding potato mixture.

Recipe from Spice and Spirit, The Complete Kosher Jewish Cookbook *by the Lubavitch Women's Cookbook Organization (New York: Bloch Publishing Co.).*

Betty Aberlin

Betty Aberlin is well loved by children for her role as Lady Aberlin, niece of the puppet King Friday the Thirteenth, on *Mister Rogers' Neighborhood.* She has entertained young audiences on *Mister Rogers* (PBS' longest running show) for over thirty years. Born in New York City, Aberlin made her stage debut at age ten in *Sandhog,* a folk opera. She originated the roles of Cheryl in *I'm Getting My Act Together and Taking It On the Road* and Mrs. Van Daan in *Yours, Anne,* a musical drama based on The Diary of Anne Frank. Aberlin has also appeared in *West Side Story* and *Guys and Dolls,* and was cast as a nun in the film *Dogma.*

"People ask me, 'Is your name Elizabeth?' 'No,' I usually reply, 'just Betty.' I am named for Bertha Kinstein, my maternal grandmother (from Russia) and the only cook in our family. In a large, pewter-colored, dented pot, she made a wonderful rice pudding with cinnamon and raisins, and soft boiled her eggs for four and a half minutes, as I still do. My grandfather, David, invented 'coffee milk,' taught me how to dunk, and ate apples, core, seeds, and all, leaving only the stem. My mother, Daisy, a single parent in days when divorce was a rarity, had to work so hard to support me and my sister Alice (of Milwaukee) that anything home-cooked was miraculous. She made apple spice cake and pineapple upside-down cake and kugel."

– Betty Aberlin

Daisy's Kugel

Kugel
3 tablespoons butter, divided
¾ pound egg noodles, boiled, drained, and rinsed
4 eggs, lightly beaten
¼ cup sugar
¼ teaspoon salt
1 pound crumbled farmer cheese or cottage cheese
¾ teaspoon cinnamon
½ cup raisins, soaked in hot water and drained
¼ teaspoon nutmeg

Topping
1 tablespoon sugar
¼ teaspoon cinnamon
2 tablespoons butter

1. **For kugel:** Preheat oven to 350°F. Using 1 tablespoon butter, grease a 9-inch square baking dish.
2. Combine eggs, sugar, salt, cheese, cinnamon, raisins, and nutmeg.
3. Cut 2 tablespoons of butter into bits. Add to egg mixture. Add noodles and mix lightly together. Transfer to prepared baking dish.
4. **For topping:** Combine cinnamon and sugar and sprinkle over noodles.
5. Dot with butter.
6. Bake 25 to 30 minutes, until top is golden.

"For latchkey children, or those with no time to spare, I recommend egg and onion matzah, spread thinly with softened butter. For me it's soul food, manna: Passover, Jerusalem, Tevye, Chagall, and the mystery of our ongoing Exodus in every flake of unleavened braille!"

Elaine Konigsburg

Elaine Konigsburg is the author/illustrator of numerous children's books, including the Newberry Medal-winning *From the Mixed-up Files of Mrs. Basil E. Frankweiler* and *The View From Saturday*. Born in New York City, she grew up in small towns in Pennsylvania, studied chemistry at Carnegie Mellon University, and attended graduate school at the University of Pittsburgh. After teaching science at a private girls' school, she began her writing career. Her three children and several of her five grandchildren have posed for illustrations in her books.

Lokchen Kugel or Jewish Pasta
from Betty Ellovich's Mother-in-Law

¼ pound butter (1 stick), melted and cooled
3 eggs, beaten
3 tablespoons sugar
1 pound creamed cottage cheese
½ pint (1 cup) sour cream
1 8-ounce can crushed pineapple, drained
8 ounces medium egg noodles, boiled and drained
4 handfuls of crushed corn flakes
3 handfuls of brown sugar

1. Preheat oven to 350°F. Grease an 11 x 7-inch or a 9-inch square pan.
2. Combine butter, eggs, sugar, cottage cheese, sour cream, pineapple, and noodles.
3. Transfer to baking dish. Top with crushed corn flakes and brown sugar.
4. Bake for 1 hour.

Susan Stamberg

Photo: Barbara Ries

Nationally renowned broadcast journalist Susan Stamberg is a special correspondent for National Public Radio. She was the first woman to anchor a nightly news program and has won every major award in broadcasting. In 1994, she was inducted into the Broadcasting Hall of Fame. Born in New York City, Stamberg earned a bachelor's degree from Barnard College. From 1972 to 1986 she co-hosted NPR's news magazine *All Things Considered*, and then hosted NPR's *Weekend Edition/Sunday* from 1987 to 1989. Stamberg is married to Louis C. Stamberg of the Department of State's Agency for International Development in Washington. They have one son, Joshua, an actor.

"My mother-in-law and I are delighted to share the recipe for the relish that sounds terrible but tastes terrific."

– ***Susan Stamberg***

Mama Stamberg's Cranberry Relish

2 cups raw cranberries
1 small onion, chopped
½ cup sugar
¾ cup sour cream
2 tablespoons horseradish

1. Grind the cranberries and onion together. Add remaining ingredients and mix. Put in a plastic container and freeze.
2. An hour before serving, move the container from the freezer to the refrigerator to thaw. The relish will be thick, creamy, and shocking pink.

Makes 1½ pints.

Charlotte Zucker

Photo: Peter Sorel

An actress in her own right, Charlotte Zucker has appeared in all of the movies directed or produced by her sons, David and Jerry Zucker, including *My Best Friend's Wedding* and the *Naked Gun* series. Born in New York City, she graduated from Brooklyn College and received a master's degree in Speech Education from the University of Wisconsin. Zucker met her husband there, and then settled in Milwaukee, where they raised three children (the Zuckers also have a daughter, Susan). In addition to her films, Zucker has been involved in teaching and theater and has been a docent at the Milwaukee Art Museum for twenty years.

"This lekvar is my mother-in-law's recipe. It was a favorite dish for our family every fall when the dark plums appeared and the peaches were ripe. It's a delicious side dish with any meal. Try it with a dollop of sour cream for a midday 'nosh.'"

– ***Charlotte Zucker***

Plum Compote

3 to 4 pounds Italian prune plums
2 peaches
1 to 2 pears
1 Macintosh apple, peeled
¾ cup (or less) sugar

1. Wash all fruit well.
2. Remove all pits, cores, and seeds, and cut into small cubes. Place fruit in a large pot.
3. Add a scant ¾ cup sugar.
4. Simmer about 2 hours, stirring frequently.

This freezes very well.

Makes about 4 cups.

Joseph Lieberman

The first Jew to be chosen as a vice presidential candidate on a major party ticket, Joseph Lieberman is also the first Orthodox Jew to serve in the U.S. Senate. The son of a shop owner, he was born and raised in Stamford, Connecticut. He received both his undergraduate and law degrees from Yale, and was elected to the Connecticut State Senate in 1970. After holding office for ten years, he served as Connecticut Attorney General from 1982 to 1988. He took office as the U.S. senator from Connecticut in 1989. His committee appointments have included the Armed Services Committee as well as the Governmental Affairs Committee. He chairs the Democratic Leadership Council. Lieberman lives with his wife, Hadassah, in New Haven. They have four children and one granddaughter.

Senator and Mrs. Lieberman's
Pistachio Rice Pilaf

¼ cup currants, plus enough warm water to cover
1 cup long-grain brown rice
2 cups vegetable broth or water
¼ cup dried apricots, cut into strips
½ cup unsalted pistachio nuts
Cinnamon

1. Soak currants for 15 minutes in warm water. Drain and set aside.
2. Wash rice and drain. Place in a skillet over medium heat and stir until rice is dry and lightly browned. Be careful not to burn it!
3. Place toasted rice in a 1½-quart saucepan and cover with 2 cups broth or water. Bring to a boil, reduce heat to low, and cover with a tight-fitting lid.
4. After rice has simmered for about 25 minutes, place the currants, apricots, and nuts on top of the rice—do not stir in. Return the lid and continue simmering 20 minutes or until rice is tender and water is absorbed. Remove from heat and let stand 2 minutes.
5. Turn into a serving dish. Sprinkle with cinnamon.

Serves 6.

Michael Dorf

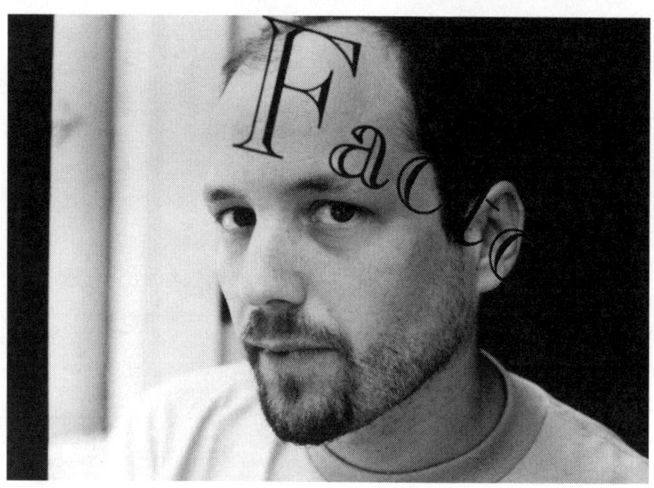

An authority on the subject of music and new technology, Michael Dorf is the owner of the Knitting Factory, a music club in lower Manhattan with a newly opened branch in Los Angeles. These facilities allow fans to hear live music in person, while reaching thousands more music lovers around the globe via the Internet, cable, and other broadband wires. Born and raised in Milwaukee, Dorf attended law school at the University of Wisconsin. In 1986, he quit school and moved to New York City, where he opened a small performance space that eventually became the Knitting Factory. Today the club hosts and produces the Bell Atlantic Jazz Festival, as well as the Intel Digital Club Festival. Dorf has pioneered a number of events, including an annual "Cyber Seder" with a virtual *haggadah*. He appears regularly on CNN, CBS, and National Public Radio.

"While some risotto purists think risotto can only be made with lobster broth and scallops, this recipe will put to good use the 'Jewish Mother' chicken soup as a base (and make my parents happy). The key to all risottos is the constant stirring required from the moment it is started until it is served. For some, this going back to Mitzraim (Egypt) or enslavement to the stove is difficult. For those with obsessive, overachieving, compulsive Jewish blood, the hypnotic stirring at the end of a long workday is bliss. With wine in one hand and a wooden spoon in the other, the process looks more difficult than it really is. More importantly, you can tune out the conversations when hosting guests, who are always impressed with the way it turns out. This meal is usually made for guests, since it takes too long to do for just yourself. The guests think you are concentrating on the risotto, but you're really enjoying some peaceful time watching grass grow and tuning your guests out."

– Michael Dorf

Dorf's Kosher Risotto

Chicken broth

1 4-pound frying chicken, cut up
2 medium onions, quartered
Lots of garlic (about 10 large cloves), peeled and halved
2 to 3 large carrots, cut in chunks
2 to 3 celery stalks, cut in chunks
2 bay leaves
10 to 12 cups water
2 teaspoons salt, or to taste
Pepper to taste

1. Combine all chicken broth ingredients in a large stockpot. Bring to a boil, cover, and reduce heat. Simmer for 2 to 3 hours, or until broth is reduced to 8 or 9 cups. Adjust salt and pepper to taste.
2. Remove chicken and vegetables, and press vegetables to release remaining liquid (save chicken for other use, if desired).
3. If you wish to remove fat, refrigerate broth until fat congeals. Remove fat from top of broth.
4. Use heated broth when making risotto.

Risotto

2 tablespoons virgin olive oil, divided
2 medium shallots, finely chopped
1 pound assorted mushrooms (shiitakes, chanterelles, buttons, morels, etc.)
Lots of garlic (about 10 cloves), chopped fine, divided
1¼ cups Arborio rice
1 cup French white burgundy (Montrachet recommended), or other dry white wine
8 to 9 cups rich chicken broth (the tastier the better)
Salt and pepper to taste
1 large bunch of parsley, chopped, for garnish

1. Heat chicken stock and keep warm.
2. In a large frying pan, heat 1 tablespoon olive oil. Add shallots, mushrooms, and half the garlic. Sauté until tender. Set aside.
3. In a large saucepan over medium heat, heat remaining tablespoon olive oil. Add remaining garlic. Just as it starts to sizzle, add rice. Stir the rice and oil for about 1 minute. Just as it starts to get dry, pour in wine and stir. Let the wine evaporate, stirring constantly. Pour in 1 cup of broth. Keep stirring—never stop. Let the rice absorb the broth. As broth is absorbed, pour in another cup of broth, stirring constantly. Continue this process until about 8 cups of broth have been added and the rice is tender but not mushy, still firm, and looks creamy (you might need to add more broth). This should take at least 20 to 35 minutes. The key is constant stirring. Add sautéed mushroom mixture (you can add some fish or other creative products) and heat through. Transfer to serving dish and cover with chopped parsley.

Serves 6.

Editor's note: For a dairy version of this recipe, use vegetable stock in place of chicken stock. Top cooked risotto with lots of freshly grated old and expensive Parmesan cheese.

Barbara Barrie

Well known for her role as Brooke Shields' "Nana" on the popular sitcom *Suddenly Susan*, Barbara Barrie has appeared in countless stage, movie, and television productions. A survivor of colon cancer, she devotes much of her time to educating the public about this disease. Barrie was born in Chicago and moved to Texas in fourth grade. She received a B.F.A. from the University of Texas at Austin and continued her acting studies in New York. Her many Broadway credits include roles in *The Prisoner of Second Avenue* and *Company*. Her performance in *The Killdeer* (with the New York Shakespeare Festival) earned her a Drama Desk and an Obie Award. Barrie played Elizabeth Miller on television's *Barnie Miller*, and her film work includes *One Potato, Two Potato*, for which she received a Best Actress Award at the Cannes Film Festival. The parents of a daughter and a son, Barrie and her husband reside on Manhattan's Upper West Side.

"For many years, in the seventies, I fell in love with Indian food. I studied it carefully, collected all the spices and made (almost) nothing else. My children, now in their thirties, used to beg me to cook one 'regular meal' occasionally or at least put some 'normal' food into the refrigerator.

A friend with whom I was doing an off-Broadway play at the time gave this green bean recipe to me. I made it the next day, and even Jane and Aaron loved it. It is very easy and goes well with roasted chicken or a full-bodied fish, or on a buffet table.

P.S. My grown-up children are now lovers of Indian food and often seek it out wherever they travel."

– Barbara Barrie

Fried Green Beans with Coconut

4 tablespoons ghee or oil
1 teaspoon black mustard seeds
½ cup chopped onion
1 teaspoon finely chopped ginger
1 teaspoon salt
½ teaspoon black pepper
1 pound green beans, cut in short pieces
¼ teaspoon red pepper
¼ cup grated dried coconut, or coconut flakes
2 tablespoons chopped fresh cilantro
2 tablespoons lemon juice

1. In wok or skillet heat oil. When oil is hot, add mustard seeds and sauté for 30 seconds.
2. Stir in onions, ginger, salt, pepper, and beans, stirring constantly. Add red pepper and stir-fry for 5 minutes.
3. Add coconut and cilantro, reduce heat to low, cover pan, and cook 10 minutes.
4. Sprinkle with lemon juice and serve.

Matt Lauer

Broadcast journalist Matt Lauer has co-anchored the popular NBC morning news program *Today* since 1997. He began his career in 1979 as a producer of the noon news in Huntington, West Virginia, where he had interned during his senior year at Ohio University. Lauer became a reporter in 1980 and went on to host news and entertainment shows in Boston, Philadelphia, and Providence. He joined *Today* in 1994, serving as a substitute anchor and news anchor before rising to his current position.

Brussels Sprouts with Maple-Orange-Walnut Butter

1 pound Brussels sprouts
1 cup (2 sticks) butter, softened
¼ cup pure maple syrup
Grated rind of 2 oranges
¼ cup toasted, chopped walnuts
Salt and pepper
Zest of 1 lemon, for garnish

1. In a medium-sized saucepan, bring salted water to a boil.
2. Clean Brussels sprouts and score them by cutting a small *x* into each stem.
3. Add Brussels sprouts to water and cook over high heat for 8 to 10 minutes, or until soft.
4. Cream butter. Add maple syrup, orange rind, walnuts, salt, and pepper, and mix well.
5. Drain Brussels sprouts and toss with butter mixture.
6. Garnish with lemon zest.

Letty Cottin Pogrebin

Writer and lecturer Letty Cottin Pogrebin was born in New York City and graduated from Brandeis University. A founder of *Ms.* magazine and its editor from 1971 to 1987, she is currently a contributing editor. Her work has appeared in numerous publications including *The New York Times*, *Washington Post*, and *Moment* magazine. Among the books she has written are *Deborah, Golda and Me: Being Female and Jewish in America* (1991) and *Getting Over Getting Older: An Intimate Journey* (1996).

Kookoo Sabzi (Persian Spinach and Green Herb Pie)

This is a wonderfully healthy, brilliantly green side dish. It perks up a plateful of brownish foods, such as meat, latkes, etc. Kosher for Passover, but great any time.

¾ cup chopped fresh mint (optional)
3 cups chopped fresh spinach leaves
2 cups chopped Italian parsley
¾ cup chopped fresh dill
6 scallions, white and green parts, chopped
¼ cup chopped cilantro (optional)
1 tablespoon corn oil or other light vegetable oil
½ to ⅔ cup matzah meal, or as needed
3 to 4 extra large eggs, or as needed, beaten lightly
1 teaspoon salt, or to taste (I use more.)
½ teaspoon white pepper, or to taste

1. Preheat oven to 350°F. Spread a thin film of oil over bottom and sides of baking dish that measures about 8 x 11½ inches.
2. Combine mint, spinach, parsley, dill, scallions, and cilantro in mixing bowl. Add oil and ½ cup matzah meal. Stir in 3 eggs and mix well with wooden spoon. Consistency should be fairly thick but slightly runny. Mixture should drop in mass from tablespoon with just a little liquid visible. Add additional egg or matzah meal, if needed, to attain that texture. Season with salt and pepper.
3. Turn egg mixture into baking dish and smooth top with back of spoon.
4. Bake for 20 to 35 minutes, or until pie is completely set and slightly shrunken away from sides of dish. Don't let it overbake or it will become dry.
5. Serve hot or cold.

Serves 8 to 10 as a side dish.

Beverly Sills
Dean Ornish
Judy Blume
Andrew Weil
Herb Kohl
Rabbi Marc Gellman
Don Rickles
Abigail Van Buren
Art Spiegelman
Joan Zakon Borysenko
Jerry Blaustein
Jerry Winkelreich
Michael Feldman
Ben Sidran
Joel Siegel
Paul Newman
Rick Moranis
Barbara Barrie
Beverly Sills
Billy Joel
Steven Spielberg
Steven Peterman
Al Clark
Faye Kellerman
Gene Weiss
Susan Isaacs
Edward Asner
Mollie Katzen
Edward Koch
Wendy Wasserstein
Robert Klein
Joey Bishop
Arlen Specter
Barbara Walters
David Zucker
Russel Feingold
Ben & Jerry
Henry Winkler
Claudia Cohen
Florence Eiseman
Susan Stamberg
Dana Goldstein
Mayim Bialik
David A. Adler
Ruth Pressler
Anita Diamant
Bethy Rutman
Ellen Evans
Bernie Siegel
Charlotte Rae
Theodore Bikel
Max Frankel
Robert Pinsky
Itzhak Perlman
Don Rickles
David H. Levy
Joan Nathan
Susan Estrich
Shecky Greene
Herb Kohl
Aaron Sorkin
Charlotte Zucker
Elaine Konigsburg
Roberta Peters
Tana Hoban
Jim Wiseman
Joseph Lieberman
Jane E. Spero
Ellen Evans

Desserts

Abigail Van Buren

Columnist, author, and lecturer Abigail Van Buren was born in Sioux City, Iowa. She is well known for her "Dear Abby" advice column, which was first published in the *San Francisco Chronicle* in 1956. Her column is now syndicated worldwide. Van Buren hosted the *Dear Abby Radio Show* from 1963 to 1975. She is the author of several books and the recipient of numerous awards for her charitable work.

Fabulous Chocolate Cake and Fluffy White Frosting

Cake

3 ounces unsweetened chocolate
½ cup (1 stick) butter
1 cup water
2 cups sifted cake flour
1¼ teaspoons baking soda
1 teaspoon salt
2 eggs
1 cup dairy sour cream (or ½ cup buttermilk)
2 cups sugar
1½ teaspoons vanilla

Fluffy Frosting

2 egg whites, at room temperature
¾ cup sugar
½ teaspoon cream of tartar
Dash of salt
2½ teaspoons water
1 teaspoon vanilla

Drizzle

1 ounce unsweetened chocolate
1 tablespoon butter

1. Preheat oven to 350°F. Grease and flour two 8-inch round cake pans.
2. **For cake:** In top of double boiler, melt chocolate, butter, and water over simmering water. Remove from heat.
3. Lightly spoon flour into measuring cup; level off. In large bowl, sift together flour, soda, and salt. Set aside.
4. In second large bowl, beat eggs and sour cream until well blended. Add sugar and vanilla; beat well. Stir in cooled chocolate mixture. Add dry ingredients, half at a time, blending at low speed just until smooth. Batter will be thin.
5. Pour batter into prepared pans. Bake for 40 minutes or until toothpick inserted in center comes out clean.
6. Cool in pans on wire racks for 10 minutes. Loosen edges with knife and invert onto cake racks. Cool completely.
7. **For frosting:** In top of double boiler, beat egg whites, sugar, cream of tartar, salt, and water until well blended. Cook over simmering water, beating constantly with electric beater, for about 7 minutes or until stiff peaks form.
8. Remove from heat and stir in vanilla. Fill and frost cake.
9. **For drizzle:** In small saucepan, melt chocolate and butter over very low heat, stirring constantly. Do not boil.
10. Drizzle over top of frosted cake, allowing chocolate to drip down sides.

Serves 12.

Francine Klagsbrun

Author Francine Klagsbrun has written many books including *Voices of Wisdom: Jewish Ideals and Ethics for Everyday Living*. She edited the best-selling *Free to Be ...You and Me*, is a columnist for *The Jewish Week* and *Moment* magazines, and has written for *The New York Times, Ms.,* and *Newsweek*. Klagsbrun lectures on social, religious, and family issues.

"Made with margarine and served without whipped cream, this flourless chocolate cake makes a perfect ending to a company meat meal. Because it has no flour, I also use it for Passover. The first time I made it, I had invited a well-known cookbook writer to my home for dinner. To my horror, after I baked the cake, the top sank and cracked. I baked a second cake to replace the first. The top sank and cracked. A third cake, same result. Out of time and energy and near tears, I showered the top with powdered sugar and cut the cake in the kitchen where guests couldn't see it. It tasted delicious, cracks and all. My cookbook friend lavished compliments on it. Feeling more confident, I confessed about my three failed attempts to make the cake look nice.

'But my dear,' she said (she's British), 'flourless cakes always crack on top.'

So don't worry if your cake sinks and cracks. It's supposed to. Just cover it with powdered sugar and lap up the compliments.”

– Francine Klagsbrun

Flourless Chocolate Cake

½ cup unsalted butter or margarine, plus extra for greasing the pan
8 ounces bittersweet chocolate, cut into small pieces
5 extra-large eggs, separated
⅛ teaspoon salt
⅔ cup sugar, divided
Powdered sugar, for garnish
Whipped cream, for serving (optional)

1. Preheat oven to 350°F. Butter and flour a 9-inch round springform pan.
2. Place butter and chocolate in the top of a double boiler over simmering water. Heat until melted, stirring occasionally. Remove from heat.
3. Set aside 3 tablespoons of the ⅔ cup sugar. In a large bowl, whisk together the egg yolks, salt, and remaining sugar. Whisk the melted chocolate into the egg yolk mixture.
4. Using an electric mixer on medium speed, beat egg whites until very foamy. Gradually beat in the reserved 3 tablespoons sugar and beat until stiff peaks form. Gently fold whites into chocolate mixture, and pour batter into prepared pan.
5. Bake cake about 45 minutes, or until toothpick inserted in center comes out clean. Let cake rest for 5 minutes before removing sides of pan. Cool. Top of cake may crack. Dust with powdered sugar and serve as is or with whipped cream.

Joan Zakon Borysenko

Photo: Michail Jang

Writer and lecturer Joan Zakon Borysenko's work integrates science, medicine, and spirituality. A licensed clinical psychologist, she completed doctoral and post-doctoral work at Harvard Medical School in cancer cell biology and behavioral medicine. Borysenko is the co-founder and former director of the Mind/Body Clinic at Beth Israel/Deaconess Hospital in Boston. Since 1988, she has been president of Mind/Body Health Sciences and gives lectures, workshops, and consultations for health care professionals, businesses, and the general public. Borysenko's many books include *Fire in the Soul, A Woman's Book of Life*, and *The New York Times* best-seller *Minding the Body, Mending the Mind.*

"My mother, Lillian Rubenstein Zakon, was born in Boston in 1909. She was a stylish flapper in her youth, and had a closet full of platform shoes saved from that era. Unfortunately, she passed away before they finally came back into style. But her recipes will never go out of style, at least while your arteries can accommodate the fat. Her culinary expertise came from four main sources: her mother, Sarah Baltimore Rubenstein; her mother-in-law, Elizabeth Berkman Zakon; a mysterious source known to me only as Mrs. Finkelstein; and the congregation *Kehillith Israel Sisterhood Cookbook*, copyright 1917. That precious tome is currently in the possession of my oldest son, Justin.

Justin, who is in the restaurant business, remembers not only his grandmother's great dishes, but also her rare kitchen disasters. He was once on a television program featuring the worst dishes that guests could remember at their family holiday dinners. Justin cooked up a plate of the apricot halves stuck together with marshmallows that his grandmother used to make on occasion. But even those weren't a total loss. He and his brother Andrei, their father, and their uncle used to toss them off the balcony as a competitive sport. They made great memories, if not great food.

One of my earliest memories is the careful preparation of desserts for Pesach. We had to tiptoe past the oven while the sponge cake baked, lest it fall. That was fine with the family, since the fallen ones were a rare treat in themselves. Mother served the sponge cakes with fresh sliced strawberries with sugar and, after she gave up keeping a kosher home, with whipped cream. Sometimes a chocolate torte or chocolate jelly roll would be served on Passover as well. I have never tasted sponge cake like hers anywhere. My mother was a true master of kitchen chemistry.”

– Joan Zakon Borysenko

Mrs. Finkelstein's Passover Chocolate Torte

9 large eggs at room temperature, separated
1½ cups sugar
5 ounces of chocolate chips (¾ cup plus 2 tablespoons), melted and cooled
3 tablespoons potato starch
1 teaspoon grated orange rind
1 cup ground walnuts
Pinch of salt

1. Preheat oven to 350°F. Grease a 10-inch tube pan with vegetable oil cooking spray.
2. Beat yolks in an electric mixer until very thick and lemon-colored.
3. Add sugar gradually while continuing to beat the yolks.
4. While still beating, add the melted chocolate.
5. Remove bowl from mixer and gently fold in potato starch, orange rind, and ground nuts.
6. Beat egg whites until foamy, add a pinch of salt, and continue beating until they hold a stiff peak.
7. Fold egg yolk mixture gently into whites and spoon into prepared pan.
8. Bake at 350°F for 10 minutes, then reduce heat to 325°F. Continue baking for another 50 minutes, or until a toothpick inserted in center comes out clean.
9. Cool for 5 minutes before inverting onto a wire rack to finish cooling.

Tana Hoban

Prizewinning filmmaker and photographer Tana Hoban was born in Philadelphia. Her photos have been exhibited at the Museum of Modern Art in New York and in galleries around the world. Her beautifully photographed children's books examine the concepts of color, shape, spatial relationships, and size. They invite readers to see everyday objects as if for the first time. Hoban's more than forty books include *Take Another Look* and *Is It Red? Is It Yellow? Is It Blue?* (both American Library Association Notable Books). She lives in Paris with her husband.

"This bundt cake recipe has always been a favourite. When my daughter was little, I baked this cake especially for her birthday. The bundt pan is so beautiful that it always made it special. It makes a great dessert, and everybody loves it."

– Tana Hoban

German Bundt Cake (Pound Cake)

Before starting cake, have all ingredients at room temperature.

1 cup butter, plus additional butter for pan
2 to 4 ounces blanched, whole almonds
1 cup granulated sugar
1 cup powdered sugar
4 egg yolks
1 teaspoon vanilla extract
1 tablespoon almond extract
4 egg whites, beaten until stiff
3 cups cake flour
2 teaspoons baking powder
Pinch of salt
1 cup milk

1. Preheat oven to 325°F. Grease 12-cup bundt pan well. Put large dabs of butter along creases of pan, embedding an almond in each dab.
2. Cream butter. Sift the 2 sugars together and add gradually to butter.
3. Add unbeaten egg yolks, one at a time, and beat until smooth. Mix in extracts.
4. Lightly spoon flour into measuring cup. Level off with a knife or other straight edge. Sift measured flour with baking powder and salt 3 times.
5. Starting and ending with flour, add flour and milk alternately to batter.
6. Fold in egg whites.
7. Pour batter into pan and bake for 1½ hours.
8. When baked, let stand 15 minutes before turning cake out of pan. Turn carefully and gently. Let cool completely before serving.

Makes 24 pieces.

Beatty Rutman

Beatty (short for Beatrice) Rutman was the mother of noted folk singer Bob Dylan, as well as a younger son, David. She and her husband, Abe Zimmerman, lived in Duluth, Minnesota, for fourteen years, where their sons were born. The family moved to Hibbing, Minnesota, when Bob was six and David was two. After Zimmerman's death in 1968, she married Joe Rutman of St. Paul, Minnesota. Later in life, Rutman divided her time between Minnesota and Arizona. She died in January 2000 at the age of eighty-four.

"I hope you do have much success in doing your cookbook. This is a very easy recipe.

Take care—from
Beatty Rutman
Bob Dylan's mother"

Banana Chocolate Chip Loaf

1 cup sugar
½ cup (1 stick) margarine, softened
2 eggs
4 tablespoons sour cream
2 ripe bananas, mashed
2 cups flour
1½ teaspoons baking powder
½ teaspoon baking soda
1 cup (6 ounces) chocolate chips

1. Preheat oven to 325°F. Generously grease two 8 x 4 x 2½-inch loaf pans.
2. Cream sugar and margarine together until fluffy. Add eggs and beat until well blended.
3. Add sour cream and bananas.
4. In another bowl mix flour, baking powder, and baking soda. Add chocolate chips to mixture.
5. Fold flour mixture into batter. Transfer batter to prepared baking pans and bake for 40 minutes.

Ben Cohen and Jerry Greenfield

Ice cream mavens Ben and Jerry met in seventh-grade gym class and became best friends. They had many things in common, including a love of good food and the fact that they were the only students who couldn't run a mile in seven minutes. When Ben later got a summer job driving an ice cream truck, he convinced Jerry to do the same. Jerry quit after one day. They went off to college. Ben dropped out and worked a number of different jobs. When Jerry was denied admission to medical school for the second time, they decided to go into business together. They settled in Burlington, Vermont, and took a fourteen-week correspondence course in ice cream making. After purchasing and renovating an old gas station, they opened Ben & Jerry's on May 5, 1978. Today, Ben & Jerry's is sold nationwide and abroad. The company is known for donating 7.5 percent of pretax earnings to charity and maintaining a "double bottom line" dedicated to earning a profit and promoting social good.

Chocolate Chip Cookie Dough Ice Cream

The idea of using raw dough may not sound very appealing, but as those who have trouble keeping their fingers out of the cookie dough know, the taste is terrific.

½ recipe (1½ cups) raw Giant Chocolate Chip Cookie Dough
Sweet Cream Base
2 teaspoons vanilla extract

1. Chop the cookie dough into bite-sized pieces, place in a bowl, cover, and freeze.
2. Prepare the sweet cream base. Add the vanilla extract and blend.
3. Transfer the mixture to an ice cream maker and freeze following the manufacturer's instructions.
4. When the ice cream is quite stiff (about 1 minute before it is done), add the chopped cookie dough. Be sure to wait until the very last moment, otherwise the dough will get sticky and unmanageable. Continue freezing until the ice cream is ready.

Makes 1 generous quart.

Giant Chocolate Chip Cookies

We like our chocolate chip cookies moist, chunky, and big—at least 3 inches across. A small ice cream scoop of dough will bake to about the right size. Of course, you don't have to bake the dough, you can use it instead to make a batch of Chocolate Chip Cookie Dough Ice Cream. If you have leftover cookies, chop them into small pieces and add to any flavor of homemade ice cream.

½ cup (1 stick) butter at room temperature
¼ cup granulated sugar
⅓ cup firmly packed brown sugar
1 large egg*
½ teaspoon vanilla extract
1 cup plus 2 tablespoons all-purpose flour
½ teaspoon salt
½ teaspoon baking soda
1 cup semisweet chocolate chips
½ cup coarsely chopped walnuts

1. Preheat oven to 350°F.
2. In a large mixing bowl, beat butter and both sugars until light and fluffy. Add egg and vanilla extract and mix well.
3. Mix flour, salt, and baking soda in another bowl. Add dry ingredients to the batter and mix until well blended. Stir in chocolate chips and walnuts.
4. Drop dough by small ice cream scoops (1 ounce or about 2 tablespoons) 2 to 3 inches apart on an ungreased cookie sheet. Flatten each scoop with the back of a spoon to about 3 inches in diameter.
5. Bake until the centers are still slightly soft to the touch, 11 to 14 minutes. Let cool on cookie sheet for 5 minutes, then transfer to racks to cool completely.

Makes 12 to 15 cookies.

**Editor's note: If using recipe for cookie dough ice cream, use ¼ cup liquid egg substitute or 2 tablespoons milk in place of egg.*

Sweet Cream Bases for Chocolate Chip Cookie Dough Ice Cream

Listed below are three options for the sweet cream base needed for Chocolate Chip Cookie Dough Ice Cream. Choose the one that you like best.

Option 1: This, our most popular base, has a creamy texture, medium body, and a subtle, understated taste. It's especially good as a background for fruit, cookies, and candy.

2 large eggs or ½ cup liquid egg substitute**
¾ cup sugar
1 cup milk
2 cups heavy or whipping cream

1. Beat eggs, sugar, and milk in top half of a double boiler. Whisk or stir continuously over gently simmering water until temperature reaches 160°F or mixture just begins to thicken. Remove top pan from heat and cool to room temperature.
2. Pour in the cream and whisk to blend. Chill until very cold or overnight before transferring to ice cream maker.

Makes 1 quart.

***If using liquid egg substitute:*
1. *Whisk egg substitute in a mixing bowl until light and fluffy, 1 to 2 minutes. Whisk in sugar, a little at a time, then continue whisking until completely blended, about 1 minute more.*
2. *Pour in the cream and milk and whisk to blend.*

Option 2: This simple recipe is made with a minimum of ingredients and requires no cooking. It makes a very creamy ice cream with 25 percent butterfat, but it does not store well in home freezers, so be prepared to eat it all.

2 cups heavy or whipping cream
¾ cup sugar
⅔ cup half-and-half

Pour cream into a mixing bowl. Whisk in sugar, a little at a time, then continue whisking until completely blended, about 1 minute more. Pour in half-and-half and whisk to blend.

Makes 1 quart.

Option 3: This recipe makes a less creamy, less rich ice cream. Ben likes the slightly "cooked" flavor of the sweetened condensed milk.

2 cups light cream
1 cup sweetened condensed milk, cold

Whisk light cream and sweetened condensed milk together in a mixing bowl until blended.

Makes 1 quart.

Russell D. Feingold

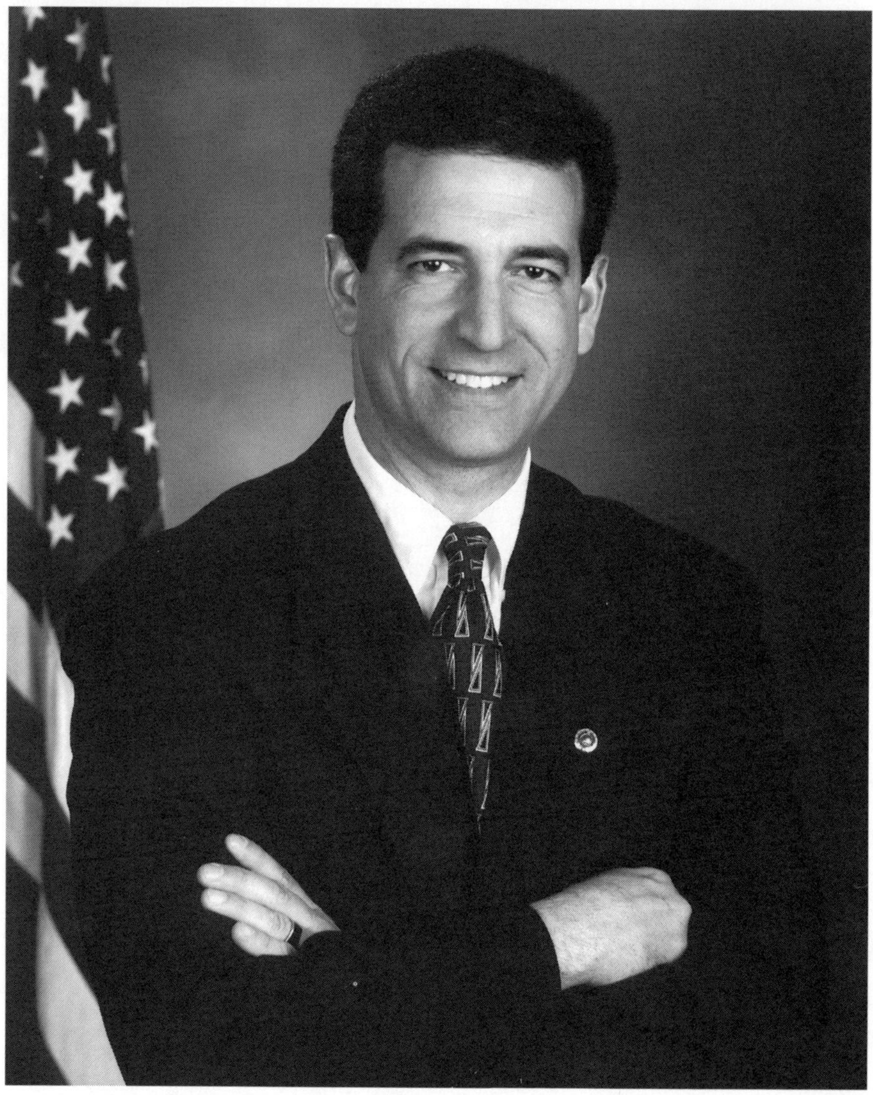

U.S. Senator Russell D. Feingold is a native of Janesville, Wisconsin. He was first elected to the U.S. Senate in 1992, having served ten years previously in the Wisconsin State Senate. A graduate of the University of Wisconsin and Harvard Law School, Feingold also attended Oxford University as a Rhodes Scholar. He lives in Middleton, Wisconsin. He is married to Mary, a freelance writer, and has two daughters and two stepsons.

This recipe comes (via Feingold's mother, Sylvia) from Hannah Sorkin, who was the wife of the Feingolds' family physician. The Sorkin and Feingold families frequently celebrated Jewish and other holidays together, and Hannah's real New York cheesecake was often featured. Mrs. Sorkin was famous for this cake, which she brought to synagogues and bake sales. As a young boy, Feingold was more a fan of pie than cheesecake for dessert. He did not believe that Hannah's cheesecake could be better than a slice of pie. She was, however, able to convince him to try a slice, and he was hooked. It has since become one of his favorite desserts—right next to pie!

Hannah's Cheesecake

Crust
26 graham crackers (2¼-inch squares), crushed
½ cup (1 stick) butter, melted

Filling
2 8-ounce packages cream cheese, at room temperature
¾ cup sugar
3 eggs, well beaten
1 teaspoon vanilla

Topping
2 cups sour cream
1 teaspoon vanilla
4½ tablespoons sugar

1. Preheat oven to 375°F.
2. **For crust:** Mix graham cracker crumbs with butter and place in bottom and up sides of a springform pan.
3. **For filling:** Whip cream cheese with sugar. Add eggs and vanilla and beat. Pour into crust.
4. Bake for 20 minutes or until firm.
5. Remove from oven and let cool for 1 hour.
6. Preheat oven to 475°F.
7. **For topping:** Whip sour cream, vanilla, and sugar until fluffy. Pour onto cake and bake for 7 minutes, or until firm.
8. Cool to room temperature. Refrigerate until cold. Remove from refrigerator approximately 1 hour before serving.

Tom Lantos

Representative Tom Lantos' odyssey from Europe to America was a remarkable one. Born in Budapest, he was forced into slave labor when the Nazis invaded Hungary in 1944. Lantos escaped to an apartment that had been placed under the protection of the Swedish government by Raoul Wallenberg. Lantos risked his life to deliver money, food, and medicine to Wallenberg's network of safe houses, in which thousands of Jews were hidden. At war's end, Lantos discovered that, with the exception of an aunt, his entire family had perished. He arrived in the U.S. in 1947, married his childhood friend Annette in 1950, and taught at San Francisco State for thirty years. Lantos has represented California in Congress since 1980. As a result of his experiences, he is a staunch supporter of the oppressed and has co-chaired the Congressional Human Rights Caucus since 1983.

Annette Lantos'
Hungarian Rhapsody Dessert

Crust
1 cup (2 sticks) melted butter
½ cup powdered sugar
2 cups flour

Filling
1½ cups (3 sticks) butter or margarine
1⅓ cups sugar, divided
8 eggs, separated
3 teaspoons lemon juice or vanilla
⅓ cup flour
2 8-ounce packages cream cheese
Powdered sugar, for serving

1. Preheat oven to 350°F.
2. **For crust:** Mix melted butter, sugar, and flour. Pat into a 9 x 13-inch oven-proof, glass baking dish. Bake 20 minutes or until crust is golden at the edges. Remove from oven (leave oven on).
3. **For filling:** Cream butter with 1 cup sugar. Add egg yolks, one at a time, beating well after each addition. Add lemon juice or vanilla.
4. Add flour and cream cheese. Cream until smooth.
5. Beat egg whites until foamy. Continue beating, gradually adding ⅓ cup sugar until soft peaks form.
6. Fold half of whites into egg yolk mixture; when blended, add remainder of whites. Pour into half-baked crust.
7. Bake 35 to 45 minutes or until knife inserted near center comes out clean (no large particles sticking).
8. Dust with powdered sugar. Cut into small squares.

May be frozen.

Serves 18 to 22.

Theodore Bikel

The multitalented Theodore Bikel has starred on stage, screen, and television, and has recorded numerous albums. Born in Vienna, he left with his family for Palestine in 1937. He apprenticed with the Habimah Theatre in Tel Aviv from 1942 to 1944 and continued his theatrical training at London's Royal Academy of Dramatic Art. Bikel created the role of Baron von Trapp in the Broadway smash hit *The Sound of Music* and has played Tevye (in *Fiddler on the Roof*) over sixteen hundred times. He made his film debut in *The African Queen* in 1951 and has demonstrated his versatility in a variety of film roles, from a Russian submarine captain in *The Russians Are Coming* to the manager of a rock group in Frank Zappa's *2000 Motels*. His recordings include *Yiddish Theatre and Folk Songs* and *Rise Up and Fight—Songs of Jewish Partisans*. Bikel has also found time to be an Amnesty International board member, a presidential appointee to the National Council on the Arts, and a senior vice president of the American Jewish Congress. He and his wife have two sons.

"Toward the end of my *Fiddler* tour, the cast published a cookbook to be sold for charity. It was called *The Oy of Cooking*. Each cast member was asked to contribute a recipe. I wavered between two recipes, chicken soup or apple crisp. This recipe did not make it into the other book, so here it is now."

– Theodore Bikel

Apple Crisp

8 medium-sized, tart apples, such as Granny Smith, peeled, cored, and sliced
Dried cranberries (optional)
¾ cup flour
1 cup brown sugar
1 teaspoon cinnamon
½ cup butter
¼ teaspoon salt

1. Preheat oven to 350°F.
2. Spread apples in an unbuttered 2-quart glass baking or casserole dish. If using cranberries, scatter liberally on top of apples.
3. For topping, combine remaining ingredients with a pastry blender or fingers until pea-sized crumbs form.
4. Scatter the topping evenly over fruit and bake for 50 to 55 minutes.

Johanna Hurwitz

Born in New York City, Johanna Hurwitz received degrees from Queens College and Columbia University. A former children's librarian, she is the author of many popular books for young readers, including *Class Clown* and *A Llama in the Family*. Hurwitz enjoys cooking and won first prize for her blackberry jam at a county fair in Vermont. She also took top honors in a nationwide rice recipe contest sponsored by Uncle Ben's. Hurwitz lives with her husband in Great Neck, New York, and Wilmington, Vermont. They have two grown children.

"Twenty-four years ago, when I moved into my home, my friend Caroline Feller Bauer mailed the recipe for Blueberry Kuchen to me. 'This is a housewarming gift,' she wrote.

It seemed a strange gift until I made the recipe for the first time. It was wonderful. Since then, every summer when blueberries are in season, I make Blueberry Kuchen. Guests and family all agree it is delicious.

The other housewarming gifts are gone: towels worn out, dishes broken. But the printed word endures! It was indeed a special and lasting gift."

– Johanna Hurwitz

Blueberry Kuchen

Crust
1 cup flour
1 pinch salt
2 tablespoons sugar
½ cup (1 stick) butter, at room temperature
1 tablespoon white vinegar

Filling
1 cup sugar
2 tablespoons flour
½ teaspoon cinnamon
3 cups fresh or frozen blueberries, divided*
1 tablespoon powdered sugar

1. Preheat oven to 400°F.
2. **For crust:** Combine flour, salt, and sugar. Work in butter with fingers or pastry cutter until large clumps form. Mix in vinegar.
3. Spread dough on bottom and ½ inch up the sides of a 9-inch loose bottom or springform pan.
4. **For filling:** Combine sugar, flour, and cinnamon, and mix with 2 cups fresh blueberries. Pour into crust. Bake 35 to 45 minutes or until blueberries are bubbling.
5. Remove from oven and top with remaining cup of blueberries. Cool.
6. Remove rim from pan and place cake on plate. Dust with powdered sugar.

**Editor's note: If using frozen blueberries, make the following modifications:*

1. Preheat oven to 350°F. Press crust into a 9-inch springform pan. Bake unfilled crust for 10 minutes. Remove from oven and raise oven temperature to 400°F.
2. Combine filling ingredients using 3 cups frozen berries and an additional 1 tablespoon flour. Pour filling into crust and bake 35 to 45 minutes or until berries are bubbling. Proceed with step 5.

Florence Eiseman

Her designs are included in the Smithsonian and Metropolitan Museum collections. Her talent won her the Neiman-Marcus Award for Distinguished Contribution to Fashion in 1955 (she shared the podium with Grace Kelly and Pierre Balmain). The name Florence Eiseman became synonymous with quality in children's fashion, and she led the industry from Milwaukee for over forty years.

What began as a hobby to quiet her nerves after the birth of her second son had turned into a multi-million dollar enterprise by the time of her death in 1988. Eiseman began sewing in the early '30s, making smocked dresses, which she designed as gifts for the children of friends. In 1945, her husband, Laurence, took a dozen organdy styles to Marshall Field's in Chicago, and the first big sale was made. Her two sons, Laurence Jr. and Robert, joined her in running the business and are still involved in the company.

The child-friendly styles, clean colors, fine fabrics, simple lines, appliqués, and whimsy combined to win many awards. Garments were designed to "let children be children" and sometimes even grow with the child. The Eiseman company produced elegant children's clothes that were worn by President Kennedy's children, Hank Greenberg's children, and well-dressed children throughout the country.

"Internationally famous children's clothing designer Florence Eiseman was not known as a cook. In fact, she was a frequent patron of restaurants where she usually consumed charred hamburgers and drank J&B scotch with seltzer and a twist of lemon. We grandchildren have no memory of her ever bringing a dish to pass at a family get-together, so this recipe is the only one passed down in her name. Florence Eiseman's Blueberry Kuchen is like her designs—classic!"

– ***Marge Eiseman,*** ***Florence's granddaughter***

Blueberry Kuchen

Crust
1 cup flour
½ cup (1 stick) butter
¼ cup granulated or powdered sugar
1 egg yolk (optional)

Topping*
1 to 2 pints blueberries (or other fruit)
Sugar
Flour
Butter

1. Preheat oven to 375°F.
2. **For crust:** Mix ingredients together until large clumps form.
3. Pat evenly into the bottom and up the sides of an 8- or 9-inch square oven-proof glass baking dish.
4. **For topping:** Mix fruit, sugar, and flour. Pour evenly over crust. Dot with butter.
5. Bake 30 minutes until crust is golden and fruit is bubbling on top.

Kuchen can also be made with other fruits. Moist fruits such as raspberries or peaches require more flour.

Editor's note: Our testers used the following quantities:

4 cups blueberries
⅓ cup sugar, or to taste
1 tablespoon flour
1 to 2 tablespoons butter

Arlen Specter

U.S. Senator from Pennsylvania Arlen Specter was born in Wichita, Kansas. He attended the University of Oklahoma and received a law degree from Yale University. In 1964 he was appointed assistant counsel for the Warren Commission, and began his term in the Senate in 1981. He has served on the Appropriations Committee and the Labor, Health and Human Services Committee. He is a recipient of the Youth Services Award from B'nai Brith.

"This recipe for a Caramel Pineapple Cake Roll is from my wife, Joan. This is one of my favorite recipes, and I hope that you enjoy it as much as I have through the years."

– Arlen Specter

Joan Specter's
Caramel Pineapple Cake Roll

Cake
Butter or margarine for greasing pan
2 8-ounce cans crushed pineapple, drained
½ cup packed dark brown sugar
¾ cup cake flour
1 teaspoon baking powder
¼ teaspoon salt
4 large eggs, separated
¾ cup sugar
2 teaspoons vanilla
1 teaspoon grated lemon rind
1 to 2 tablespoons powdered sugar

Frosting
1 cup heavy or whipping cream
3 tablespoons powdered sugar

1. **For cake:** Preheat oven to 375°F.
2. Generously grease bottom and sides of a 10 x 15-inch jelly roll pan.
3. Spread drained fruit evenly over bottom of pan and sprinkle with brown sugar.
4. Sift flour with baking powder and salt.
5. Beat egg whites until foamy and add sugar gradually, beating until stiff.
6. Beat yolks into stiffened whites and add vanilla and lemon rind. Sprinkle flour over batter and gently fold in.
7. Spoon batter on top of pineapple and spread evenly.
8. Bake 18 to 20 minutes or until browned.
9. While cake bakes, sprinkle a clean, non-terry towel with water to dampen.
10. Remove cake from oven and loosen edges with a knife. Place towel on top of hot cake and invert cake onto towel. Remove pan. Sprinkle cake lightly with powdered sugar.
11. Using towel as an aid, roll cake (do not roll towel into cake). Allow cake to cool to room temperature in towel.
12. **For frosting:** While cake cools, whip heavy cream with powdered sugar until stiff.
13. When cake is cool, remove from towel, place on platter, and frost.

Joel Siegel

Joel Siegel, television's *Good Morning America* film critic since 1981, has also been a freelance writer for *The Los Angeles Times* and *Rolling Stone* magazine, a joke writer for Senator Robert Kennedy, and author of *The First.* He is the founding president of Gilda's Club, a nonprofit support center for cancer patients and their families. Siegel's varied roles have been rewarded with six New York Emmy Awards, the Public Service Award from the Anti-Defamation League of B'nai Brith, a Tony Award nomination, and the New York Associated Press Broadcasters Award for "general excellence in individual reporting."

Fruit Cobbler

Fruit Filling
8 large, ripe peaches (3 to 4 pounds), pitted and sliced
1½ cups light brown sugar
1 teaspoon apple pie spice
Juice of ½ lemon
1 tablespoon instant tapioca (optional)
2 tablespoons raspberry liqueur (optional)
4 tablespoons unsalted butter

Dough
2 cups sifted flour
2 teaspoons baking powder
½ teaspoon baking soda
6 tablespoons unsalted butter, softened
1½ cups buttermilk
Whipped cream (optional)

1. Preheat oven to 425°F. Generously grease a 12-inch oven-proof frying pan or a 13 x 9 x 2-inch baking pan.
2. **For filling:** Place peaches, brown sugar, apple pie spice, lemon juice, tapioca, and raspberry liqueur in large bowl. Mix and let macerate for approximately 10 minutes.
3. Put into pan. Dot with butter.
4. Bake for 20 to 25 minutes.
5. **For cobbler:** Sift dry ingredients into a mixing bowl. Mix in butter with your hands until flour is the consistency of oatmeal. Add buttermilk to flour mixture and stir.
6. When peaches are done, use a large spoon to drop the batter onto the peaches. Do not mix. The batter will expand.
7. Bake an additional 25 minutes or until biscuits are golden brown. Allow to cool slightly. Serve while still warm with fresh whipped cream.

Cobbler Filling Alternative 1
2 to 3 quarts blueberries, blackberries, or huckleberries
1½ cups sugar
Juice of ½ lime
Zest of ½ lime
1 tablespoon tapioca (optional)

Cobbler Filling Alternative 2
4 pounds plums, each cut into 8 pieces, or 3 to 4 pounds sliced nectarines
1½ cups light brown sugar
Juice of ½ lemon

Joan E. Spero

Photo: Wagner Inter.

Joan E. Spero is president of the Doris Duke Charitable Foundation, the 25th largest foundation in the United States. Prior to that, she served as U.S. Undersecretary of State for Economic, Business and Agricultural Affairs in the first Clinton administration. She was also a vice president at American Express and one of three U.S. ambassadors to the United Nations. Born and raised in Milwaukee, she holds a degree from the University of Wisconsin.

"Everyone loves these tasty, but not heavy, pies. They have been served to diplomats, bankers, and politicians."

– Joan E. Spero

Aunt Joan's Summer Connecticut Fruit Pie

2 unbaked 9-inch pie crusts, made from scratch or frozen
8 to 10 cups peaches, Italian plums, apples, or any fresh fruit in season (peeled or unpeeled), cut into chunks. Blueberries, cranberries or walnuts may be added.
½ cup (1 stick) butter or margarine, melted
1 tablespoon flour
⅔ cup sugar, or to taste
1 egg, beaten
Ice cream or heavy cream, for serving (optional)

1. Preheat oven to 425°F.
2. Divide fruit evenly between the 2 pie crusts.
3. Add flour and sugar to melted butter. Stir thoroughly and cool.
4. Add egg and mix well.
5. Pour butter mixture over fruit.
6. Bake 20 minutes.
7. Reduce heat to 350°F and bake an additional 40 minutes or until fruit is bubbling over most of pie surface.
8. Let cool.

Serve with ice cream or heavy cream poured on top.

Editor's note: If using frozen fruit, bake pie an additional 10 to 15 minutes.

Max Frankel

Former *New York Times* executive editor Max Frankel was born in Germany and came to the U.S. in 1940. Educated at Columbia University, he began his career at *The Times* in 1952. He won a Pulitzer Prize for international reporting in 1973 and served as executive editor from 1986 to 1994. He is the author of *The Times of My Life: And My Life With the Times*, an account of his newspaper career. His wife, Joyce Purnick, is former Metro editor of *The New York Times* and writes the "Metro Matters" column.

"I have always loved my mother's Passover sponge cake. It's light and airy, great with strawberries for dessert or toasted for breakfast—so good that I ordered it year round.

One year, when Mary Frankel was too weak to bake, my wife, Joyce Purnick, asked for the recipe. Mom went to her recipe file—a small metal box with recipes written on 3 x 5-inch index cards—pulled one out, and this is all it said:

1½ cups sugar
1 lemon rind
9 eggs
½ glass orange juice
1 cup matzah cake meal
¼ cup potato starch
1 tablespoon oil

There were no instructions, and when Joyce asked for them, Mom replied something like, 'You make it like any other sponge cake!'

It took a search through a few cookbooks to fill in the blanks."

– Max Frankel

Mom's Sponge Cake

9 eggs, separated
1½ cups sugar
½ glass orange juice (4 to 5 tablespoons)
Rind of 1 lemon, grated
1 tablespoon oil
1 cup matzah cake meal
¼ cup potato starch

1. Preheat oven to 325°F. Grease an angel food cake pan.
2. Beat egg yolks until frothy and lemon-colored, using an eggbeater or an electric mixer.
3. Add sugar gradually, then add orange juice, grated lemon rind, and oil.
4. Sift together cake meal and potato starch, and add to egg yolk mixture.
5. Beat egg whites until stiff and shiny, but not dry. Gently fold in other ingredients.
6. Pour into pan and bake for about an hour.
7. Remove from oven. Invert pan and cool thoroughly before removing cake from pan.

Claudia Roden

Photo: Martin Brigdale

Food writer Claudia Roden was born and raised in Cairo, Egypt. Uprooted by the 1956 war between Israel and Egypt, she migrated to London, where she lives today. Roden has traveled extensively around the world, gathering stories and recipes for her work. Her many cookbooks include *The Book of Jewish Food: An Odyssey from Samarkand to New York*, winner of an IACP/Julia Child Award.

"Amandines (almond balls) are little sweet treats that we made as children in Egypt. When our parents got together to prepare special goodies for the Jewish holidays, the children took part by rolling the almonds into balls or making bracelets with dough. When I make these today, I always think of the happy times in Egypt before my extended family was dispersed all over the world."

– Claudia Roden

Amandines (Almond Balls)

2 cups ground almonds
½ cup powdered or superfine sugar, plus a little more for rolling the balls in at the end
3 tablespoons rose or orange blossom water
About 12 blanched almonds or pistachio nuts to garnish

1. Mix ground almonds and sugar in a bowl and add rose or orange blossom water. Work well with hands. The mixture will seem dry at first, but the almonds will release enough oil to bind it. Knead to a soft dough.
2. Roll into 1-inch balls (the size of large marbles), then roll in sugar and decorate each by placing an almond or a pistachio nut on top.

Makes about 12 balls.

Ellen Bravo

A nationally-recognized expert on working women's issues, Ellen Bravo is co-director of 9 to 5, National Association of Working Women. Established in 1973, 9 to 5 is the nation's largest nonprofit membership organization of working women. Since becoming co-director in 1993, Bravo has worked to continue its mission of ending sexual harassment and discrimination and winning better wages, working conditions, and family-friendly policies for women. Bravo is the author of *The Job/Family Challenge: A 9 to 5 Guide* and co-author of *The 9 to 5 Guide to Combating Sexual Harassment.* She and her husband, Larry Miller, have two sons.

"These were our family favorites. Enjoy!"

– Ellen Bravo

Brownies

2 ounces of unsweetened chocolate
½ cup (1stick) butter
1 cup sugar
2 eggs
¾ cup flour
½ teaspoon salt
½ teaspoon baking powder
1 teaspoon vanilla extract

1. Preheat oven to 350°F. Grease a 9-inch square pan.
2. Melt the chocolate and butter over moderately low heat. Remove from heat.
3. Stir in sugar, eggs, and flour, stirring well after adding each ingredient. Add salt, baking powder, and vanilla.
4. Pour batter into pan and bake for 30 minutes.

Joan Nathan

Photo: Murray Bognovitz

Joan Nathan was born in Providence, Rhode Island. Her mother's parents, who came from Galicia, Austria-Hungary, and Cracow, Poland, were part of the great immigration of Eastern European Jewry. Her father left Augsburg, Germany, for the United States in 1929. Nathan is the nationally acclaimed author of many cookbooks, including *Jewish Cooking in America,* which won the Julia Child Award for Best Cookbook of the Year in 1994 from the International Association of Culinary Professionals, as well as the 1994 James Beard Award for Food of the Americas. *The Jewish Holiday Baker* (1997) introduces thirteen bakers and their recipes from around the world. She hosted *Jewish Cooking in America with Joan Nathan,* a twenty-six-part series for PBS.

"When I was a little girl, my Aunt Lisl always made butter cookies at Hanukkah time. We decorated them. The cookies were stored in her garage in airtight containers. Sometimes we got to take some of them home. Other times, we just nibbled them at her house.

One of the best things about cooking with relatives is that it's a great time to ask for stories. While we baked, Aunt Lisl told us wonderful tales of my father's boyhood in Germany. This is one of my all-time favorite family recipes."

– Joan Nathan

Aunt Lisl's Butter Cookies

1 cup (2 sticks) unsalted butter or margarine
¾ cup sugar
2 eggs
1 tablespoon brandy
1 teaspoon vanilla extract
⅛ teaspoon salt
3½ cups all-purpose flour
1 large egg white, slightly beaten
Sugar, for topping

1. Preheat oven to 350°F.
2. In a food processor, cream together butter and sugar. Add eggs, brandy, vanilla, and salt, and process.
3. Gradually add flour, mixing well. Place in a bowl; cover and chill at least 1 hour or overnight.
4. On a lightly floured surface, roll half the dough ⅛-inch thick. Keep remaining dough chilled while working. Cut with desired cookie cutter(s), dipping the cutter into flour between cuts to prevent sticking. Transfer cutouts to ungreased cookie sheets. Brush cutouts with egg white and lightly sprinkle with sugar. Repeat with remaining dough.
5. Bake for 10 to 12 minutes, or until cookies are golden. Remove and cool on wire racks.

Makes 4 dozen cookies.

Wendy Selig-Prieb

The only female chief executive of a major league baseball club, Wendy Selig-Prieb was named President and Chief Executive Officer of the Milwaukee Brewers in August 1998. Milwaukee-born Selig-Prieb attended Tufts University and began her baseball career in the Brewers broadcasting department in 1982. Selig-Prieb left the Brewers to earn a law degree, graduating from Marquette University Law School in 1988. After a brief stint as a corporate attorney, she returned to the Brewers as General Counsel in 1990. She and her husband, Laurel Prieb, Brewers Vice President of Corporate Affairs, have a daughter and live in Whitefish Bay, Wisconsin.

Lemon Squares

Crust
1 cup (2 sticks) butter, softened
½ cup powdered sugar
2 cups flour, unsifted
1 teaspoon salt

Filling
4 medium eggs, slightly beaten
2 cups sugar
4 tablespoons flour
1 teaspoon baking powder
½ cup fresh lemon juice
Additional powdered sugar, for serving

1. Preheat oven to 350°F.
2. Combine crust ingredients with a fork or pastry blender. Cut in butter until mixture is crumbly and size of small peas. Press mixture evenly onto bottom of ungreased 13 x 9-inch pan. Poke crust randomly with a fork.
3. Bake 15 minutes until crust begins to brown slightly.
4. Mix filling ingredients, beating until fluffy.
5. Pour filling over hot crust. Bake 20 to 25 minutes or until no imprint remains when touched lightly in center.
6. Remove from oven and sprinkle with powdered sugar.
7. Refrigerate overnight before cutting. This is an important step.
8. Cut into squares. Store in refrigerator.

Makes 24 2-inch squares.

Jane Breskin Zalben

Known for her richly detailed illustrations, children's book author Jane Breskin Zalben has written many books about Jewish holidays. She has also acted as art director and designer for a number of her books. Her popular titles include *Beni's First Chanukah*; *Happy Passover, Rosie*; and *Pearl Plants a Tree*. Born and raised in New York City, Zalben received a B.A. in art from Queens College. She began her career as a graphic designer and worked for several publishing houses, including Scribner's, where she was art director of children's books. Zalben lives with her husband and two sons in Sands Point, New York.

"Beni's grandparents love to dip mandelbrot (almond bread) in a glass of tea. 'When the dough gets a little hard the next day,' Grandma says, 'I could nearly *plotz* it's so delicious! And the almonds, heaven.' Mandelbrot is great for Shabbat because it stays fresh several days!"

– *Jane Breskin Zalben*

Editor's note: Beni is one of Zalben's book characters.

Mama's Mandelbrot

4 large eggs
1½ cups sugar
1 teaspoon vanilla extract
½ teaspoon almond extract
Pinch of cinnamon
½ cup vegetable oil
¼ teaspoon salt
3 cups unbleached white flour
1 tablespoon baking powder
¼ teaspoon grated lemon rind
½ cup whole almonds, chopped in blender or food processor
½ cup slivered almonds

1. Preheat oven to 350°F. Grease three 4½ x 9-inch loaf pans.
2. In a large bowl, beat together eggs, sugar, vanilla and almond extracts, and cinnamon.
3. Add oil and blend.
4. Into a separate bowl, sift together salt, flour, and baking powder.
5. Add grated lemon rind to dry ingredients above.
6. Gradually add dry mixture to wet. Blend thoroughly.
7. Mix chopped almonds with slivered almonds.
8. Fold nuts into dough. Pour batter into pans. Do not pour batter more than 1 inch deep in pan.
9. Bake 45 minutes.
10. Slice immediately! Cut into ½- to 1-inch slices. How thick you slice will determine the number of oblong cookies

Makes 3 loaves.

Susan Isaacs

Photo: Marion Ettlingler

Best-selling author Susan Isaacs was born in Brooklyn and educated at Queens College in New York City. Her first book, *Compromising Positions,* published in 1978 was a main selection of the Book-of-the-Month Club. This was followed by numerous novels including *Lily White* and *Red, White and Blue,* both of which were main selections of the Literary Guild. Her fiction has been translated into thirty languages. Isaacs has two children and lives on Long Island with her husband of over thirty years.

"This recipe is from my wonderful aunt, Sara Asher, who presides over the best kitchen on Long Island. Sara is the ambulatory antidote to all those loathsome, condescending "JAP" remarks. She is what a Jewish woman is: When not cooking, Sara's reading fiction and philosophy, studying—most recently tai chi and Shakespeare—traveling, going to concerts and theater. She's an incredibly warm and gracious hostess, a lively companion, and an enormously intelligent citizen. Oh yes, Sara is a grand mother (to say nothing of an awesome grandmother) and a loving wife. And on her next birthday she'll be eighty."

– Susan Isaacs

Forget the biscotti. Try
Aunt Sara's Mandelbrodt

1 cup corn, peanut, or canola oil
1 cup sugar
3 eggs
3½ cups flour
1 generous tablespoon baking powder
Dash of salt
2 teaspoons vanilla
Nuts: sliced almonds, toasted and cooled, or chopped pecans, macadamias, or walnuts*
Dried fruit: cranberries, cherries, or chopped apricots*
Or, if the mood strikes you, throw in some chocolate morsels.

1. Preheat oven to 350°F. Grease jelly roll pan.
2. Beat oil and sugar together.
3. Beat in other ingredients.
4. Knead by hand about 1 minute.
5. Divide dough into quarters and make loaves, 2½ to 3 inches wide.
6. Bake for 30 minutes.
7. Let cool, then cut into slices on diagonal (about ¾ inch thick).
8. Put back in oven on 2 sheets for 12 minutes to dry.

Makes 3 to 4 dozen pieces.

**Editor's note: Use a cup or more of nuts and/or dried fruit and/or chocolate, or divide dough into quarters and add ¼ cup of different fruits, nuts, or chocolate to each quarter.*

David A. Adler

An incredibly prolific writer, David A. Adler is the author of more than 150 books for children, including the extremely popular *Cam Jansen* series and *Child of the Warsaw Ghetto.* Born and raised in New York, he majored in economics at Queens College and earned an M.B.A. at New York University. Adler taught middle school math for almost nine years before becoming a full-time writer. He has received many honors for his work, including a Sydney Taylor Award (for excellence in Jewish children's books) in 1987 for *The Number on My Grandfather's Arm.* Adler lives with his wife and children in New York.

"I grew up in a big, old house with plenty of room for the eight of us: my parents, my three brothers, my two sisters, and me. My grandmother, who we all called 'Mutti,' German for mother, often stayed with us on Shabbat and Jewish holidays.

On Hanukkah we all played dreidel, and that meant trouble. My brother Eddie believed in doing things exactly right, and he always complained bitterly that Mutti was cheating. He was right. She did cheat at dreidel and at most games she played with us. She'd spin a *gimmel* and claim it was a *shin.* She'd spin a *hey* and claim it was a *nunn.* Mutti just wanted her grandchildren to be happy. She cheated to lose."

– *David A. Adler*

Moon Crescent Cookies

2 cups flour
¼ teaspoon salt
1 cup (2 sticks) unsalted margarine
½ cup powdered sugar
1 teaspoon vanilla
1 cup very finely chopped or ground almonds
Additional powdered sugar, for topping

1. Preheat oven to 350°F.
2. Sift flour into bowl and stir in salt. Set bowl aside.
3. In a second bowl, beat margarine with sugar and vanilla.
4. Add almonds to sugar mixture.
5. Add flour and salt to sugar mixture and stir.
6. Shape dough into crescents and place on ungreased cookie sheets.
7. Bake 12 to 15 minutes, until cookies are golden brown.
8. Immediately after taking cookies out of oven, while they are still hot, put several teaspoons of powdered sugar into a sifter and sift over cookies.

Makes about 3 dozen cookies.

Roberta Peters

A phone call in 1950 set Roberta Peters on the path to opera stardom. The singer playing Zerlina, the lead character in *Don Giovanni*, was unable to perform, and nineteen-year-old Peters was asked to take her place. Her Metropolitan Opera debut stunned both audience and critics. Known for her coloratura soprano voice, she has sung in major opera houses around the world and, after appearing with the Bolshoi Opera in Moscow, was the first American to receive the Bolshoi medal in 1972. Peters was born in New York City and began her training at age thirteen when her grandfather, a waiter at Grossinger's, asked Jan Peerce to hear her sing. Peerce was performing at the hotel and, impressed with her voice, sent her to William Hermann, who prepared her for a career in opera. Peters served a six-year term on the National Council on the Arts and was given the National Medal of Arts in 1998 by President Clinton. She has performed at a number of benefits in Israel for the Roberta Peters Scholarship Fund at Hebrew University in Tel Aviv. Peters is married and has two sons.

Toffee Cookies

1 cup butter, at room temperature
1 cup packed brown sugar
1 egg yolk
1 cup flour
9¼ ounces semisweet or milk chocolate candy bars or chocolate chips
⅔ cup chopped pecans

1. Preheat oven to 350°F. Line a 10 x 15-inch jelly roll pan with foil. Grease foil.
2. Cream butter and sugar until fluffy. Add egg yolk and mix well.
3. Add flour and stir until mixed.
4. Spread dough into pan.
5. Bake 20 minutes, or until brown.
6. Remove from oven and immediately top with chocolate. When melted, spread chocolate with a spatula. Top with pecans.
7. Cool slightly and cut on diagonal into diamond shapes. When completely cool, recut.

Bernie Siegel

A retired surgeon, Bernie Siegel writes and speaks extensively about the mind-body connection in medicine and its importance to health and well-being. He attended Colgate University and received an M.D. from Cornell University Medical College. He is the author of several books, including *Prescriptions for Living* (1998) and *Love, Medicine and Miracles* (1986). He and his wife have five children and live near New Haven, Connecticut.

"God had Adam and Eve eat from the tree of knowledge to learn they were mortal. Time is precious. When we accept our mortality, we begin to live.
As a physician, teacher, author, husband, father, and grandfather I know the power of love."

– Bernie Siegel

Life Pudding

Start with a liberal helping of love. Stir in compassion and commitment.
Sprinkle humor liberally until it meets your taste test.

Do not serve without grandparent's advice on final preparation.

Garnish with reverence and devotion.

Ice with action, wisdom, and prayer with chocolate flavoring.

Let stand until ready, then serve for a lifetime. It is low-fat and low-calorie and can be consumed in large quantities whenever you have a hunger for life.

The more you serve the better you feel. It isn't necessary to be served to feel fulfilled.

Take your lifetime preparing and savoring what you create.

Joan E. Spero
Abigail Van Buren
Jeffrey Blumstein
Art Spiegelman
Susan Estrich
Joey Bishop
Jane E. Brody
Joseph Lieberman
Beverly Sills
Judy Blume
Dean Ornish
Andrew Weil
Herb Kohl
Rabbi Marc Gellman
Joan Zaken Borysenko
Jerry Markbreit
Don Rickles
Edward Koch
Michael Feldman
Joel Siegel
Ben Sidran
Paul Newman
Rick Moranis
Barbara Barrie
Beverly Sills
Wendy Wasserstein
Billy Joel
Mandy Patinkin
Robert Klein
Steven Peterman
Al Clark
Steven Spielberg
Faye Kellerman
Barbara Walters
Edward Asner
Mollie Katzen
Nora Ephron
Jessie Davis
Susan Isaacs
Wendy Selig-Prieb
David Zucker
Russel Feingold
Matt Lauer
Tana Hoban
Ben & Jerry
Henry Winkler
Alfred Uhry
Claudia Cohen
Florence Eisman
Letty Cottin Pogrebin
Dana Goldstein
Mayim Bialik
David A. Adler
Ruth Prawer Jhabvala
Anita Diamant
Susan Stamberg
Roberta Peters
Ellen Bravo
Bernie Siegel
Beatty Rutman
Theodore Bikel
Max Frankel
Charlotte Rae
Itzhak Perlman
Robert Pinsky
David H. Levy
Joan Nathan
Shecky Greene
Aaron Sorkin
Elaine Konigsburg
Johanna Hurwitz
Charlotte Zucker
Jim Abrahams

Index

Aberlin, Betty, 112
Abrahams, Jim, 82
Adler, David A., 174
Apples
  Apple Crisp, 149
  Traditional Passover Haroset, 13
Apricots
  Pistachio Rice Pilaf, 121
  Sweet Potato Matzah Ball Tzimmes with Apricot Sauce, 101
Asner, Edward, 94
Asparagus, Warm Spring Salad, 89
Avocado, Mexican Salad, 87
Banana Chocolate Chip Loaf, 140
Barley, Soup, Mushroom and, 33
Barrie, Barbara, 124
Bars. *See* Cookies and Bars
Beans
  Fat Free Dip, 5
  Mexican Meat Mixture, 79
  Vegetarian Chili, 55
Beef
  Cabbage Borscht, 19
  Kapusniak, 23
  Mexican Meat Mixture, 79
  Pot Roast, 83
  Stuffed Cabbage Rolls, 75
  Sweet-and-Sour Meatballs, 17
  Sweet-and-Sour Stuffed Cabbage, 77
  Tongue, 85
Ben and Jerry, 141
Bialik, Mayim, 100
Bikel, Theodore, 148
Bishop, Joey, 106
Bleustein, Jeffrey, 16
Blintzes, Cheese, 57
Blueberry Kuchen, 151, 153
Blume, Judy, 46
Borscht
  Cabbage, 19
  Spinach, 36
Borysenko, Joan Zakon, 136
Bravo, Ellen, 164
Broccoli Salad Sandwich, 47
Brody, Jane E., 76
Brownies, 165
Brussels Sprouts with Maple-Orange-Walnut Butter, 127
Cabbage
  Borscht, 19
  Soup, 21
  Stuffed, Cabbage Rolls, 75
  Stuffed, Sweet-and-Sour, 77
Cakes and Kuchen
  Banana Chocolate Chip Loaf, 140
  Blueberry Kuchen, 151, 153
  Caramel Pineapple Cake Roll, 155
  Fabulous Chocolate, 133
  Flourless Chocolate, 135
  German Bundt, 139
  Hannah's Cheesecake, 145
  Hungarian Rhapsody Dessert, 147
  Mom's Sponge Cake, 161
  Passover Chocolate Torte, 137
Carrot Soup, 25
Challah, Honey Whole Wheat, 14
Cheese
  Blintzes, 57
  Cream Cheese Hors d'Oeuvres, 7
  Daisy's Kugel, 113
  Lokchen Kugel, 115
  Macaroni and, 66
  Mexican Salad, 87
  White Lasagna for Passover, 63
Cheesecake
  Hannah's, 145
  Hungarian Rhapsody Dessert, 147
Chicken
  Risotto, 123
  Salsa, 53
  Skinless Baked, 49
  Warm Spring Salad, 89
  Wisconsin Marinated, 51

Chicken Fat, to Render, 3
Chicken Livers, Very Fattening Chopped, 3
Chicken Soup
  Grandma Dorothy's, 27
  Risotto with, 123
Chili, Vegetarian, 55
Chocolate
  Banana Chocolate Chip Loaf, 140
  Brownies, 165
  Cake, Fabulous, 133
  Cake, Flourless, 135
  Chocolate Chip Cookies, 142
  Passover Torte, 137
  Toffee Cookies, 177
Clark, Al, 48
Coconut, Fried Green Beans with, 125
Cohen, Ben, 141
Cookies and Bars
  Amandines, 163
  Brownies, 165
  Butter, Aunt Lisl's, 167
  Chocolate Chip, 142
  Lemon Squares, 169
  Mandelbrot, Mama's, 171
  Mandelbrodt, Aunt Sara's, 173
  Moon Crescent, 175
  Toffee, 177
Corn Chips
  Mexican Meat Mixture, 79
  Mexican Salad, 87
Cranberries
  Relish, 117
  Sauce, with Sweet and Sour Meatballs, 17
Cream Cheese Hors d'Oeuvres, Hot, 7
Cucumber, Grilled Tuna and Marinated Salad, 45
Dear Abby, 132
Diamant, Anita, 96
Dip, Fat Free Bean, 5
Dorf, Michael, 122
Dylan, Bob, 140
Eggs
  Cheese Blintzes, 57
  "Dutch Babies" Pancake, 59
  Joanne's Hollandaise Sauce, 41
  Matzah Brei, 61
Eiseman, Florence, 152
Ephron, Nora, 70
Estrich, Susan, 20
Feingold, Russell, 144
Feldman, Michael, 34
Fish
  Gefilte, 9
  Gefilte, Indian Style, 11
  Salmon, Succulent Blackened Shabbos, 43
  Scrod, Dilled Fillets of, 41
  Tuna, Grilled and Marinated Cucumber Salad, 45
Frankel, Max, 160
Frosting, Fluffy White, 133
Fruit. *See also* specific fruits
  Cobbler, 157
  Pie, Summer Fruit, 159
Gazpacho, Summer, 29
Gefilte Fish, 9
Gefilte Fish, Indian Style, 11
Gellman, Rabbi Marc, 14
Goldstein, Darra, 104
Green Beans, Fried with Coconut, 125
Greene, Shecky, 18
Greenfield, Jerry, 141
Haroset, Traditional Passover, 13
Hoban, Tana, 138
Hollandaise Sauce, 41
Honey
  Challah, Honey Whole Wheat, 14
  Haroset, Traditional Passover, 13
Hurwitz, Johanna, 150
Ice Cream, Chocolate Chip Cookie Dough, 142
Isaacs, Susan, 172
Jhabvala, Ruth Prawer, 10
Joel, Billy, 44
Judge Judy Sheindlin, 37
Katzen, Mollie, 108
Kellerman, Faye, 52
Klagsbrun, Francine, 134
Klein, Robert, 102
Koch, Edward, 28
Kohl, Herb, 50
Konigsburg, Elaine, 114

Kugel
- Daisy's, 113
- Lokchen, 115
- Potato, 107
- Potato Zucchini, 111
- Tante Malka's Potato Deluxe, 109

Lady Aberlin, 112
Lantos, Tom, 146
Lasagna, White Passover, 63
Latkes, Sweet Potato, 99
Lauer, Matt, 126
Lemon Squares, 169
Lentil Soup, 31
Lettuce, Mexican Salad, 87
Levis, Jesse, 110
Levy, David H., 78
Lieberman, Joseph, 120
Liver, Chopped Chicken, 3
Macaroni and Cheese, 66
Mandelbrodt, Aunt Sara's, 173
Mandelbrot, Mama's, 171
Markbreit, Jerry, 68
Matzah
- Brei, 61
- White Lasagna, 63

Matzah Ball, Sweet Potato Tzimmes, 101
Meatballs, Sweet and Sour, 17
Moranis, Rick, 60
Mushrooms
- Mushroom Barley Soup, 33
- Risotto, 123
- Tongue and Sauce, 85
- Warm Spring Salad, 89

Nathan, Joan, 166
Newman, Paul, 40
Noodles. *See* Pasta
Nuts
- Amandines, 163
- Chocolate Chip Cookies, 142
- German Bundt Cake, 139
- Haroset, Traditional Passover, 13
- Mandelbrodt, Aunt Sara's, 173
- Mandelbrot, Mama's, 171
- Moon Crescent Cookies, 175
- Passover Chocolate Torte, 137
- Pistachio Rice Pilaf, 121
- Potato Pancake, 105
- Toffee Cookies, 177

Ornish, Dean, 54
Osso Buco, 81
Pancake(s)
- "Dutch Babies," 59
- Potato (*Labda*), 105

Passover
- Amandines, 163
- Flourless Chocolate Cake, 135
- Haroset, 13
- Kookoo Sabzi (Spinach and Green Herb Pie), 129
- Matzah Brei, 61
- Mom's Sponge Cake, 161
- Chocolate Torte, 137
- Sweet Potato Latkes, 99
- Sweet Potato Matzah Ball Tzimmes, 101
- White Lasagna, 63

Pasta/Noodles
- Daisy's Kugel, 113
- Lokchen Kugel, 115
- Macaroni and Cheese, 66
- Spaghetti Casserole, 69
- Spaghetti with Sand, 71

Patinkin, Mandy, 6
Peaches, Fruit Cobbler, 157
Perlman, Itzhak, 2
Peterman, Steven, 64
Peters, Roberta, 176
Pie, Summer Fruit, 159
Pineapple
- Caramel Pineapple Cake Roll, 155
- Lokchen Kugel, 115

Pinsky, Robert, 4
Pistachio Rice Pilaf, 121
Plum Compote, 119
Podwal, Mark, 26
Pogrebin, Letty Cottin, 128
Potatoes
- Balsamic Roasted, 95
- Hungarian, 103
- Kugel, 107
- Kugel Deluxe, 109
- Pancake (*Labda*), 105
- Potato Zucchini Kugel, 111
- Trio of Roasted Potatoes, 97

Potatoes, Sweet. *See* Sweet Potatoes
Pot Roast, 83
Rae, Charlotte, 8
Raichlen, Steven, 98
Reinsdorf, Jerry, 90
Relish, Cranberry, 117
Rice
  Pistachio Rice Pilaf, 121
  Risotto, 123
  Sweet-and-Sour Stuffed Cabbage, 77
  Warm Spring Salad, 89
Rickles, Don, 62
Risotto, 123
Roden, Claudia, 162
Rutman, Beatty, 140
Salad
  Grilled Tuna and Marinated Cucumber, 45
  Mexican, 87
  Warm Spring, 89
Salmon, Blackened, 43
Sauerkraut, Kapusniak, 23
Scrod, Dilled Fillets, 41
Selig-Prieb, Wendy, 168
Sheindlin, Judge Judy, 37
Sidran, Ben, 30
Siegel, Bernie, 178
Siegel, Joel, 156
Sills, Beverly, 58
Skibell, Joseph, 42
Sorkin, Aaron, 12
Soup
  Cabbage, 21
  Cabbage Borscht, 19
  Carrot, 25
  Chicken Broth, with Risotto, 123
  Chicken, Grandma Dorothy's, 27
  Gazpacho, 29
  Kapusniak, 23
  Lentil, 31
  Mushroom Barley, 33
  Spinach Borscht, 36
Spaghetti. *See* Pasta
Specter, Arlen, 154
Spero, Joan E., 158
Spiegelman, Art, 22
Spielberg, Steven, 56
Spinach
  Borscht, 36
  Kookoo Sabzi (Spinach and Green Herb Pie), 129
Sponge Cake, 161
Stamberg, Susan, 116
Steinem, Gloria, 24
Stew, Brunswick, 73
Sweet Potatoes
  Latkes, 99
  Matzah Ball Tzimmes, 101
  Trio of Roasted Potatoes, 97
Taus, Ellen, 88
Tomatoes
  Gazpacho, 29
  Salsa Chicken, 53
Tongue with Sauce, 85
Tuna, Grilled and Marinated Cucumber Salad, 45
Turkey
  Brunswick Stew, 73
  Mexican Meat Mixture, 79
Uhry, Alfred, 72
Uris, Leon, 80
Van Buren, Abigail, 132
Veal, Osso Buco, 81
Vegetables
  Broccoli Salad Sandwich, 47
  Brussels Sprouts with Maple-Orange-Walnut Butter, 127
  Cabbage Soup, 21
  Carrot Soup, 25
  Green Beans, Fried with Coconut, 125
  Gazpacho, 29
  Kookoo Sabzi (Spinach and Green Herb Pie), 129
  Potato Zucchini Kugel, 111
  Spinach Borscht, 36
Vegetarian Main Dishes
  Broccoli Salad Sandwich, 47
  Cheese Blintzes, 57
  Chili, 55
  "Dutch Babies" Pancake, 59
  Macaroni and Cheese, 66
  Matzah Brei, 61
  Mexican Salad, 87
  Spaghetti Casserole, 69

- Spaghetti with Sand, 71
- White Lasagna, 63

Walters, Barbara, 74
Wasserstein, Wendy, 67
Weil, Andrew, 32
Whole Wheat Challah, 14
Wine
- Dilled Fillets of Scrod, 41
- Haroset, 13
- Osso Buco, 81
- Risotto, 123
- White Lasagna, 63

Winkler, Henry, 86
Zalben, Jane Breskin, 170
Zucchini, Potato Kugel, 111
Zucker, Charlotte, 118
Zucker, David, 84

Beverly Sills
Dean Ornish
Judy Blume
Herb Kohl
Andrew Weil
Rabbi marc Gellman
Abigail Van Buren
Art Spiegelman
Joan Zakon Borysenko
Don Rickles
Judy Body
Michael Feldman
Edward Koch
Ben Sidran
Joel Siegel
Donalee Patinkin Rubin
Beverly Sills
Paul Newman
Rick Moranis
Barbara Barrie
Wendy Wasserstein
Billy Joel
Mandy Patinkin
Robert Klein
Steven Spielberg
Steven Peterman
Al Clark
Faye Kellerman
Leon Uris
Susan Isaacs
Mollie Katzen
Nora Ephron
Barbara Walters
Wendy Selig-Prieb
David Zucker
Russel Feingold
Tana Hoban
Ben & Jerry
Henry Winkler
Florence Eiseman
Susan Stamberg
Steven Peterman
Joan Natnan
Dana Goldstein
Marjorie Biolik
David A. Adler
Ellen Bravo
Roberta Peters
Bernie Siegel
Charlotte Rae
Theodore Bikel
Itzhak Perlman
Don Rickles
Joan Natnan
Robert Pinsky
Susan Estrich
Shecky Greene
Aaron Sorkin
Herb Kohl
Elaine Konigsburg
Charlotte Zucker
Theodore Bikel
Joan E. Spero
Jim Abrahams
Joseph Lieberman
Jane E. Brody
Ellen Pava
Abigail Van Buren
Beverly Sills
Judy Blume
Don Rickles
Dean Ornish
Joan Zakon Borysenko
Andrew Weil
Michael Feldman
Joel Siegel
Ben Sidran
Rick Moranis
Barbara Barrie

To order

To order by check

(no cash, please)

Please send $18.00 per book *(payable to MJDS)* plus shipping and handling* to:

Milwaukee Jewish Day School
Attn: Cookbook
6401 N. Santa Monica Blvd.
Milwaukee, WI 53217

Please include your name and address, shipping address *(if different)* a daytime phone number *(with area code)*, and indicate the number of books you would like to receive.

*Shipping and handling costs are:
$4.00 for the first book plus $2.00 for each additional book sent to the same address
$4.00 for each book sent to a different address

To order by credit card

please call (toll-free) 1-877-763-1569

For additional information, you may visit our web site at
www.mjds.org/cookbook or call our toll-free cookbook line at
1-877-763-1569

All proceeds from the sale of this book benefit Milwaukee Jewish Day School.